chain-free CROCHET

INTRODUCTION
CHAIN-FREE CROCHET

If you took a survey of crochet lovers and asked them what their least favorite thing about crochet was, you would probably get a variety of answers: dye lots that don't match *(a fact you don't discover until you are halfway through an afghan)*, pull skeins you can't find the end of, tucking in the thousands of tail ends of yarn in a multicolored project. But there is one thing that most crocheters almost universally dislike: the starting chain. The world may never know how many budding crocheters simply gave up after being instructed to "ch 89, dc in 4th ch from hook, dc in each ch across." Simple though it may seem, actually working all those stitches into all those chains can be a daunting task. Questions like, "Does the loop on my hook count as a chain?" and "Do I put my hook under one loop of

the chain or two?" and "I know I counted the right number of chains; why don't I have enough to finish the row?" plague the novice crocheter and cause frustration and discouragement. Experienced crocheters may advise others to work the chain loosely, or to use a larger hook size for the chain, but these helpful tips may cause the starting edge of the item to look loose and sloppy. If only there was a way to bypass this tedious chore!

But all crochet projects start with a chain—right? Wrong! In *Chain-Free Crochet*, you will find over 19 different ways to start your next crochet project, no matter if it is a row of V-stitches or a round of double crochets!

The marvelously versatile foundation stitches allow you to make both the starting chain

and the first row of stitches at the same time. The lacy eyelet foundation makes starting either rows or rounds easy and fun to do. The slip ring eliminates the center hole when working in rounds. But these are just the beginning! We have also included chain-free foundations for popular stitches such as V-stitches, shells and filet spaces. Our easy chain-free love knot foundation blends in so beautifully with the rest of the design, you won't be able to tell which end is which!

Innovative crochet designer Belinda "Bendy" Carter has developed several amazing foundations, including a cast-on single crochet foundation which is similar to the slingshot method of casting on in knitting. Bendy uses this method to start her stunning All Knit-Look Sweater.

TABLE OF **CONTENTS**

Chain-Free Crochet

Imagine a technique that allows you to make the foundation chain and the stitches of the first row at the same time! Called foundation stitches, this little-known technique is easy and fun to do, allowing you to work exactly the number of stitches needed for the first row of your pattern. Foundation stitches make the first row more elastic, and the edge has a neat, finished appearance. The basic idea for single crochet, half double crochet, double crochet and treble crochet foundation stitches is the same; once you understand the idea behind it, you will be able to work any stitch with ease.

NOTE: Unless otherwise stated, always insert hook through 2 lps of the base chain.

1. Single crochet foundation stitch (sc foundation st):
Ch 2, insert hook in 2nd ch from hook, yo, pull lp through, yo, pull through 1 lp on hook *(base ch completed)* yo, pull through 2 lps on hook *(sc completed)*;

Next st: Insert hook in base ch just completed, yo, pull lp through (see photo 1a), yo, pull through 1 lp on hook *(base ch completed)*, yo, pull through 2 lps on hook (see photo 1b). Rep until desired number of sts have been completed (see photo 1c).

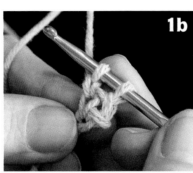

2. Half double crochet foundation stitch (hdc foundation st):
Ch 2, yo, insert hook in 2nd ch from hook, yo, pull lp through, yo, pull through 1 lp on hook *(base ch completed)*, yo, pull through last 3 lps on hook *(hdc completed)*;

Next st: *Yo, insert hook in last base ch completed (see photo 2a), yo, pull lp through, yo, pull through 1 lp on hook *(base ch)* (see photo 2b), yo, pull through all 3 lps on hook, rep from * until desired number of sts have been completed (see photo 2c).

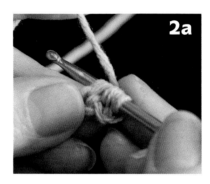

3. Double crochet foundation stitch (dc foundation st):

Ch 3, yo, insert hook in 3rd ch from hook, yo, pull lp through, yo, pull through 1 lp on hook *(base ch completed)*, yo, pull through 2 lps on hook, yo, pull through last 2 lps on hook *(dc completed)*;

Next st: *Yo, insert hook in last base ch completed (see photo 3a), yo, pull lp through, yo, pull through 1 lp on hook *(base ch)* (see photo 3b), yo, pull through 2 lps on hook (see photo 3c), yo, pull through last 2 lps *(dc completed)*, rep from * until desired number of sts have been completed (see photo 3d).

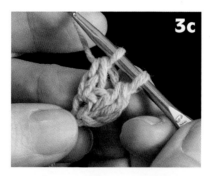

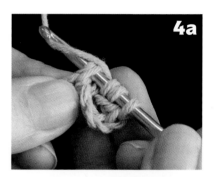

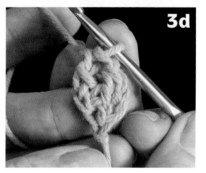

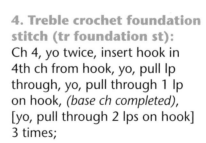

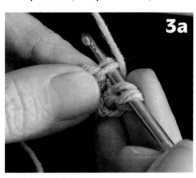

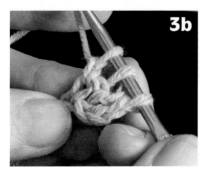

4. Treble crochet foundation stitch (tr foundation st):

Ch 4, yo twice, insert hook in 4th ch from hook, yo, pull lp through, yo, pull through 1 lp on hook, *(base ch completed)*, [yo, pull through 2 lps on hook] 3 times;

Next st: *Yo twice, insert hook in last base ch completed (see photo 4a), yo, pull lp through, yo, pull through 1 lp on hook (see photo 4b), [yo, pull through 2 lps on hook] 3 times, rep from * until desired number of sts have been completed (see photo 4c).

But what if the first row of your pattern calls for something other than a solid row of stitches? You can also use this concept to make a variety of stitches for your foundation, including chain spaces. This is done by yarning over 1 extra time for each chain stitch you need before you do your yarn overs for the next stitch. These extra yarn overs will be worked off to make chain spaces between the foundation stitches.

5. Double crochet with chain-1 foundation (dc, ch-1 foundation): This will give you a foundation of dc's with ch-1 sps between them:

Ch 4, yo twice, insert hook in 4th ch from hook, yo, pull lp through, yo, pull through 2 lps on hook *(ch sp completed)*, yo, pull through 1 lp on hook *(base ch completed)*, [yo, pull through 2 lps on hook] twice *(dc completed)*;

Next st: *Ch 1, yo twice, insert hook in last base ch completed (see photo 5a), yo, pull lp through, yo, pull through 2 lps on hook (see photo 5b), yo,

pull through 1 lp on hook (see photo 5c), [yo, pull through 2 lps on hook] twice, rep from * for desired number of sts (see photo 5d).

6. Small V-stitch foundation (small V-st foundation): This will give you a foundation of (dc, ch 1, dc) V-sts with a ch-2 sp between their bases;

Ch 4, dc in 4th ch from hook *(first small V-st completed)*, *yo 3 times, insert hook in same ch last V-st was worked in (see photo 6a), yo, pull lp through, [yo, pull through 2 lps on hook] twice *(2 chs completed)* (see photo 6b), yo, pull through 1 lp on hook *(base ch completed)* (see photo 6c), [yo, pull through 2 lps on hook] twice (see photo 6d), ch 1, yo, insert hook in last base ch completed, yo, pull lp through (see photo 6e), [yo, pull through 2 lps on hook] twice *(small V-st completed)*, rep from * until desired number of sts have been completed (see photo 6f).

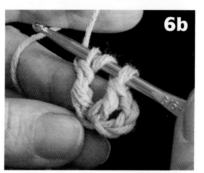

Chain-Free Crochet

7. Large V-stitch foundation (large V-st foundation): This will give you a foundation of (dc, ch 2, dc) V-sts with a ch-3 sp between their bases;

Ch 5, dc in 5th ch from hook *(first large V-st completed)*, *yo 4 times, insert hook in same ch last large V-st was worked in (see photo 7a), yo, pull lp through, [yo, pull through 2 lps on hook] 3 times *(3 chs completed)* (see photo 7b), yo, pull through 1 lp on hook *(base ch completed)* (see photo 7c), [yo, pull through 2 lps on hook] twice (see photo 7d), ch 2, yo, insert hook in last base ch completed, yo, pull lp through (see photo 7e), [yo, pull through 2 lps on hook] twice, rep from * until desired number of sts have been completed (see photo 7f).

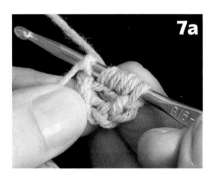

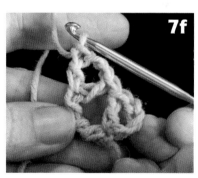

8. Open shell foundation:
This will give you a foundation of
(2 dc, ch 2, 2 dc) shells with
a ch-3 sp between their bases;

Ch 4, (dc, ch 2, 2 dc) in 4th
ch from hook, *yo 4 times,
insert hook in same ch last shell
was worked in (see photo 8a),
yo, pull lp through, [yo, pull
through 2 lps on hook] 3 times
(3 chs completed) (see photo
8b), yo, pull through 1 lp on
hook *(base ch completed)* (see
photo 8c), [yo, pull through 2
lps on hook] twice (see photo
8d), (dc, ch 2, 2 dc) in last base
ch completed, rep from * until
desired number of sts have been
completed (see photo 8e).

9. Solid shell foundation:

This will give you a foundation of alternating sc and 5 dc shells with ch-2 sps between their bases;

Ch 2, insert hook in 2nd ch from hook, yo, pull lp through, yo, pull through 1 lp on hook *(base ch completed)*, yo, pull through 2 lps on hook *(sc completed)*, *yo 3 times, insert hook in last base sc completed (see photo 9a), yo, pull lp through, [yo, pull through 2 lps on hook] twice (see photo 9b), yo, pull through 1 lp on hook *(base ch completed)* (see photo 9c), [yo, pull through 2 lps on hook] twice *(dc completed)* (see photo 9d), work 4 more dc in last base ch completed (see photo 9e), yo twice, insert hook in last base ch completed, yo, pull lp through, [yo, pull through 2 lps on hook] twice (see photo 9f), yo, pull through 1 lp on hook *(base ch completed)* (see photo 9g), yo, pull through 2 lps on hook *(sc completed)*, rep from * until desired number of sts have been completed (see photo 9h).

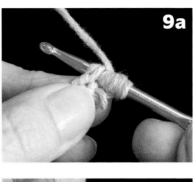

10. Slip ring: Leaving 4-inch end on yarn, lap yarn over 4-inch end forming lp, insert hook through lp from front to back, yo *(see step 1 of Fig. 1)* (see photo 10a), pull through lp to form ring, yo, pull through lp on hook *(see step 2 of Fig. 1)* (see photo 10b).

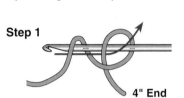

Step 1

4" End

Step 2

Leave ring loose until stitches are made.

Slip Ring Foundation Stitch Fig. 1

10a

10b

11. Rolled ring: Wrap yarn several times around 1 or more fingers to adjust size of center (see photo 11a). Slide yarn off finger or fingers, sl st or sc in ring (see photo 11b). Complete according to instructions.

11a

11b

12. Double crochet eyelet (dc eyelet): [Ch 3, dc in 3rd ch from hook] number of times stated (see photo 12).

12

13. Treble crochet eyelet (tr eyelet): [Ch 4, tr in 4th ch from hook] number of times stated (see photo 13).

13

14. Love knot foundation:
Ch 2, sc in 2nd ch from hook
(see photo 14a), pull up 1-inch
long lp on hook (see photo 14b),
yo, pull through lp (see photo
14c) sc in back strand of long
lp (see photo 14d).

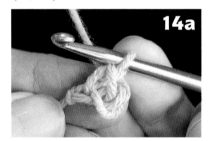

**15. Bendy's slingshot cast on
knit:** Holding end in front
of hook and skein in back of
hook (see photo 15a), wrapping
yarn around finger using
slingshot cast on *(see Fig. 1)*,
slide lp off finger onto hook,
(cast on 1 st) (see photo 15b), yo
from skein going from back over
hook and to back again, pull
through both lps on hook, 1 st
completed (see photo 15c).

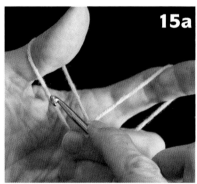

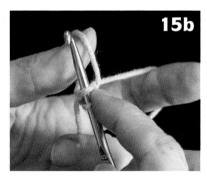

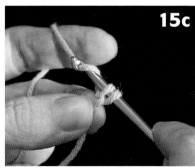

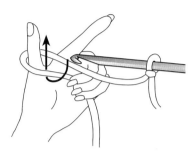

**Slingshot Cast On
Fig. 1**

**16. Single crochet twist
(sc twist):** Ch 2, sc in 2nd ch
from hook, turn (see photo 16a),
ch 1, sc in last sc made, turn
(see photo 16b).

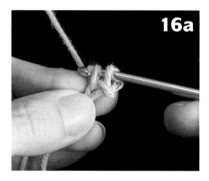

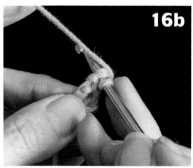

17. Puff stitch foundation st (puff st foundation st): Ch 1, *pull up ½ lp, [yo, insert hook in ch, yo, pull through pulling up ½-inch lp] twice (see photo 17a), yo pull through all lps on hook, ch 1, rep from * number of times stated (see photo 17b).

18. Bendy's cast on: Place slip knot on hook, hold end in front of hook, hold skein in back of hook (see photo 18a), yo with end going from front over hook and back to front *(2 lps on hook)* (see photo 18b), yo with skein going from back over hook and back to back, pull through 1 lp on hook *(2 lps on hook)* (see photo 18c), yo with skein going from back over hook and back to back, pull through both lps on hook *(st completed)* (see photo 18d).

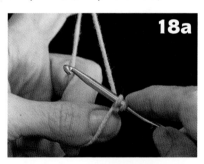

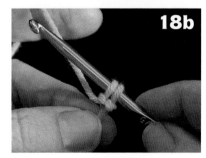

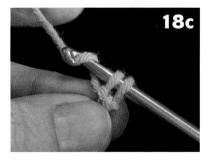

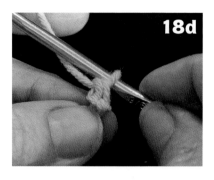

19. Back bar single crochet (back bar sc): Ch 1, sc in back bar of ch (see photo 19a), rep for number of sc needed (see photo 19b).

DESIGN BY ELIZABETH ANN WHITE

SKILL LEVEL

EASY

FINISHED SIZE

5¼ x 6¼ inches

MATERIALS

- Elmore-Pisgah Peaches & Crème medium (worsted) weight cotton yarn (2½ oz/122 yds/71g per ball):
    1 ball #56 celery
- Size H/8/5mm crochet hook

GAUGE

Gauge for this project is not important.

FOUNDATION STITCH

Single crochet foundation stitch (sc foundation st): Ch 2, insert hook in 2nd ch from hook, yo, pull lp through, yo, pull through 1 lp on hook *(base ch completed)* yo, pull through 2 lps on hook *(sc completed);*

Next st: Insert hook in base ch just completed, yo, pull lp through, yo, pull through 1 lp on hook *(base ch completed),* yo, pull through 2 lps on hook. Rep until desired number of sts have been completed.

INSTRUCTIONS
HOT PAD

Row 1: Work **sc foundation st** *(see Foundation Stitch)* 25 times, turn. *(25 sc)*

Row 2: Ch 1, sc in first st, [ch 1, sk next st, sc in next st] across, turn.

Rows 3–20: Ch 1, sc in first st, [ch 1, sk next ch sp, sc in next st] across, turn.

Row 21: Ch 1, sc in first st, [sc in next ch sp, sc in next st] across. Fasten off. ●

SINGLE-CROCHET FOUNDATION
QUICK STITCH PULLOVER

DESIGN BY MARGARET HUBERT

SKILL LEVEL

BEGINNER

FINISHED SIZES
Instructions given fit women's small; changes for medium, large and X-large are in [ ].

FINISHED GARMENT MEASUREMENTS
Bust: 36 inches *(small)* [40 inches *(medium)*, 44 inches *(large)*, 48 inches *(X-large)*]

MATERIALS
- Bernat Softee Chunky bulky (chunky) weight yarn (3½ oz/164 yds/100g per ball):
    5 [5, 6, 7] balls #39008 natural
- Size P/15mm crochet hook or size needed to obtain gauge
- Tapestry needle

GAUGE
2 sts = 1 inch

Take time to check gauge.

PATTERN NOTES
Front and Back are worked from side to side.

Chain-1 at beginning of row or round counts as first single crochet unless otherwise stated.

FOUNDATION STITCH
Single crochet foundation stitch (sc foundation st): Ch 2, insert hook in 2nd ch from hook, yo, pull lp through, yo, pull through 1 lp on hook *(base ch completed)* yo, pull through 2 lps on hook *(sc completed)*;

Next st: Insert hook in base ch just completed, yo, pull lp through, yo, pull through 1 lp on hook *(base ch completed)*, yo, pull through 2 lps on hook. Rep until desired number of sts have been completed.

INSTRUCTIONS
PULLOVER
BACK
Row 1: Work 41 [42, 43, 44] **sc foundation sts** *(see Foundation Stitch)*, turn.

Row 2: Ch 1 *(see Pattern Notes)*, working in **back lps** *(see Stitch Guide)*, sc in each st across to last st, working in both lps, sc in last st, turn.

Next rows: Rep row 2 until piece measures 18 [20, 22, 24] inches from beg. At end of last row, fasten off.

FRONT
Work same as Back.

SLEEVE
Make 2.

Row 1: Work 32 [34, 36, 38] sc foundation sts, turn.

Row 2: Ch 1, working in back lps, sc in each st across to last st, working in both lps, sc in last st, turn.

Next rows: Rep row 2 until piece measures 19 [19½, 20, 20½] inches from beg. At end of last row, fasten off.

FINISHING
Sew 4 [4½, 5, 5½] inches of ends of rows on Front and Back tog on each edge for shoulder seams. This will leave 10 [11, 12, 13] inches open for neck opening.

Mark Back and Front 8 [8½, 9, 9½] inches down from shoulder seam for Sleeve placement

Fold 1 Sleeve in half lengthwise, place fold at shoulder seam, sew in place between markers.

Rep with rem Sleeve.

Sew side and Sleeve seams, leaving last 4 inches on Sleeve unsewn.

Sew 4-inch seam on each Sleeve with RS tog so the seam is on the RS of work.

Fold 4 inches up on each Sleeve for cuff. Tack in place if desired. ●

HALF DOUBLE CROCHET FOUNDATION **HOT PAD**

DESIGN BY ELIZABETH ANN WHITE

SKILL LEVEL

EASY

FINISHED SIZE
5¼ x 6¼ inches

MATERIALS
• Elmore-Pisgah Peaches & Crème medium (worsted) weight cotton yarn (2½ oz/ 122 yds/71g per ball):
   1 ball #13 burnt orange
• Size H/8/5mm crochet hook

GAUGE
Gauge for this project is not important.

PATTERN NOTE
Chain 2 at beginning of row or round counts as first half double crochet unless otherwise stated.

FOUNDATION STITCH
Half double crochet foundation stitch (hdc foundation st): Ch 2, yo, insert hook in 2nd ch from hook, yo, pull lp through, yo, pull through 1 lp on hook (base ch completed), yo, pull through last 3 lps on hook (hdc completed);

Next st: *Yo, insert hook in last base ch completed, yo, pull lp through, yo, pull through 1 lp on hook (base ch), yo, pull through all 3 lps on hook, rep from * until desired number of sts have been completed.

INSTRUCTIONS
HOT PAD
Row 1: Work **hdc foundation st** (see Foundation Stitch) 26 times, turn. (26 hdc)

Rows 2–11: Ch 2 (see Pattern Note), [sk next st, hdc in next st, hdc in st just sk] across, ending with hdc in last st, turn.

Row 12: Ch 2, hdc in each st across. Fasten off. ●

HALF DOUBLE CROCHET FOUNDATION **ARAN AFGHAN**

DESIGN BY SHIRLEY BROWN

SKILL LEVEL

INTERMEDIATE

FINISHED SIZE
53 x 67 inches, excluding Fringe

MATERIALS
- Medium (worsted) weight yarn: 66 oz/3,300 yds/ 1,871g Aran
- Size G/6/4mm crochet hook or size needed to obtain gauge

GAUGE
5 post sts = 1 inch; 1 post st row = 1 inch

FOUNDATION STITCH
Half double crochet foundation stitch (hdc foundation st): Ch 2, yo, insert hook in 2nd ch from hook, yo, pull lp through, yo, pull through 1 lp on hook *(base ch completed)*, yo, pull through last 3 lps on hook *(hdc completed)*;

Next st: *Yo, insert hook in last base ch completed, yo, pull lp through, yo, pull through 1 lp on hook *(base ch)*, yo, pull through all 3 lps on hook, rep from * until desired number of sts have been completed.

SPECIAL STITCHES
2-treble crochet cross-stitch (2-tr cross-st): Sk next 2 sts, tr in each of next 2 sts, working behind 2 sts just made, tr in first sk st, tr in next sk st.

3-treble crochet back cross-stitch (3-tr back cross-st): Sk next 3 sts, tr in each of next 3 sts, working behind sts made, tr in first sk st, tr in each of next 2 sk sts.

3-treble crochet front cross-st (3-tr front cross-st): Sk next 3 sts, tr in each of next 3 sts, working in front of sts just made, tr in first sk st, tr in each of next 2 sk sts.

Cluster (cl): Holding back on hook last lp of each st, 4 tr in next ch sp, yo, pull through all lps on hook.

INSTRUCTIONS
AFGHAN

Row 1: Work **hdc foundation st** (see Foundation Stitch) 125 times, turn. (125 hdc)

Row 2: Ch 1 (does not count as a st), hdc in first st and in each st across, turn.

Row 3: Ch 1, dc in each of first 4 sts, [ch 1, sk next st, dc in next st] 3 times, dc in each of next 4 sts, **2-tr cross-st** (see Special Stitches), dc in each of next 2 sts, 2-tr cross-st, dc in next st, **fptr** (see Stitch Guide) around each of next 9 sts, dc in next st, fptr around next st, dc in next st, [**3-tr back cross-st** (see Special Stitches), dc in next st, fptr around next st, dc in next st, **3-tr front cross-st** (see Special Stitches), dc in next st, fptr around next st, dc in next st] 3 times, fptr around each of next 9 sts, dc in next st, 2-tr cross-st, dc in each of next 2 sts, 2-tr cross-st, dc in each of next 5 sts, [ch 1, sk next st, dc in next st] 3 times, dc in each of last 3 sts, turn.

Row 4: Ch 1, dc in each of first 4 sts, **cl** (see Special Stitches) in next ch sp, dc in next st, dc in next ch sp, dc in next st, cl in next ch sp, dc in each of next 5 sts, 2-tr cross-st, dc in each of next 2 sts, 2-tr cross-st, dc in next st, **bptr** (see Stitch Guide) around each of next 9 sts, dc in next st, bptr around next st, dc in next st, [3-tr back cross-st, dc in next st, bptr around next st, dc in next st, 3-tr front cross-st, dc in next st, bptr around next st, dc in next st] 3 times, bptr around each of next 9 sts, dc in next st, 2-tr cross-st, dc in each of next 2 sts, 2-tr cross-st, dc in each of next 5 sts, cl in next ch sp, dc in next st, dc in next ch sp, dc in next st, cl in next ch sp, dc in each of last 4 sts, turn.

Row 5: Ch 1, dc in first st, fptr around each of next 2 sts, dc in next st, [ch 1, sk next st, dc in next st] 3 times, fptr around each of next 2 sts, dc in each of next 2 sts, 2-tr cross-st, dc in each of next 2 sts, 2-tr cross-st, dc in next st, fptr around each of next 9 sts, dc in next st, fptr around next st, dc in next st, [3-tr back cross-st, dc in next st, fptr around next st, dc in next st, 3-tr front cross-st, dc in next st, fptr around next st, dc in next st] 3 times, fptr around each of next 9 sts, dc in next st, 2-tr cross-st, dc in each of next 2 sts, 2-tr cross-st, dc in each of next 2 sts, fptr around each of next 2 sts, dc in next st, [ch 1, sk next st, dc in next st] 3 times, fptr around each of next 2 sts, dc in last st, turn.

Row 6: Ch 1, dc in each of first 4 sts, dc in next ch sp, dc in next st, cl in next ch sp, dc in next st, dc in next ch sp, dc in each of next 5 sts, 2-tr cross-st, dc in each of next 2 sts, 2-tr cross-st, dc in next st, bptr around each of next 9 sts, dc in next st, bptr around next st, dc in next st, [3-tr back cross-st, dc in next st, bptr around next st, dc in next st, 3-tr front cross-st, dc in next st, bptr around next st, dc in next st] 3 times, bptr around each of next 9 sts, dc in next st, 2-tr cross-st, dc in each of next 2 sts, 2-tr cross-st, dc in each of next 5 sts, dc in next ch sp, dc in next st, cl in next ch sp, dc in next st, dc in next ch sp, dc in each of last 4 sts, turn.

Rows 7–74: [Rep rows 3–6 consecutively] 17 times.

Rows 75 & 76: Rep rows 3 and 4.

Rows 77 & 78: Ch 1, hdc in each st across, turn. At end of last row, fasten off.

FRINGE
Cut 2 strands, each 15 inches long. Holding both strands tog, fold in half, insert hook in end of row, pull fold through, pull all ends through fold, tighten. Trim ends.

Attach Fringe in each st across each short end of Afghan. ●

DOUBLE CROCHET FOUNDATION HOT PAD

DESIGN BY ELIZABETH ANN WHITE

SKILL LEVEL

EASY

FINISHED SIZE
5¼ x 6 inches

MATERIALS
- Elmore-Pisgah Peaches & Crème medium (worsted) weight cotton yarn (2½ oz/122 yds/71g per ball):
  1 ball #52 light sage
- Size H/8/5mm crochet hook

GAUGE
Gauge for this project is not important.

PATTERN NOTE
Chain-3 at beginning of row or round counts as first double crochet, unless otherwise stated.

FOUNDATION STITCH
Double crochet foundation stitch (dc foundation st): Ch 3, yo, insert hook in 3rd ch from hook, yo, pull lp through, yo, pull through 1 lp on hook *(base ch completed)*, yo, pull through 2 lps on hook, yo, pull through last 2 lps on hook *(dc completed)*;

Next st: *Yo, insert hook in last base ch completed, yo, pull lp through, yo, pull through 1 lp on hook *(base ch)*, yo, pull through 2 lps on hook, yo, pull through last 2 lps *(dc completed)*, rep from * until desired number of sts have been completed.

INSTRUCTIONS
HOT PAD
Row 1: Work **dc foundation st** *(see Foundation Stitch)* 24 times, turn. *(25 dc)*

Rows 2–8: Ch 3 *(see Pattern Note)*, dc in **back lps** *(see Stitch Guide)* of each of next 3 sts, [dc in **front lps** *(see Stitch Guide)* of each of next 4 sts, dc in back lps of each of next 4 sts] twice, dc in front lps of each of last 4 sts, turn.

Row 9: Ch 3, dc in each st across. Fasten off. ●

SKILL LEVEL

EASY

FINISHED SIZE
13½ inches square

MATERIALS
- Lion Brand Cotton-Ease medium (worsted) weight yarn (3½ oz/207 yds/100g per skein):

    2 skeins #122 taupe
    1 skein each #194 lime, #134 terra-cotta and #186 maize
- Size H/8/5mm crochet hook or size needed to obtain gauge
- Sewing needle
- Taupe sewing thread

GAUGE
7 dc = 2 inches;
2 dc rows = 1 inch

PATTERN NOTE
Chain-3 at beginning of row or round counts as first double crochet, unless otherwise stated.

FOUNDATION STITCH
Double crochet foundation stitch (dc foundation st):
Ch 3, yo, insert hook in 3rd ch from hook, yo, pull lp through, yo, pull through 1 lp on hook *(base ch completed)*, yo, pull through 2 lps on hook, yo, pull through last 2 lps on hook *(dc completed);*

Next st: *Yo, insert hook in last base ch completed, yo, pull lp through, yo, pull through 1 lp on hook *(base ch)*, yo, pull through 2 lps on hook, yo, pull through last 2 lps *(dc completed)*, rep from * until desired number of sts have been completed.

SPECIAL STITCH
Shell: 5 dc as specified.

INSTRUCTIONS
BAG
Row 1: With taupe, work **dc foundation st** *(see Foundation Stitch)* 40 times, turn.

Rnd 2: Now working in rnds, ch 3 (see Pattern Note), dc in each st across, 5 dc in end of row 1, working in opposite side of Foundation, dc in each st across, 5 dc in end of row 1, join with sl st in 3rd ch of beg ch-3. *(90 dc)*

Rnd 3: Working in **back lps** *(see Stitch Guide)*, ch 3, dc in each st around, join with sl st in 3rd ch of beg ch-3.

Rnds 4–6: Ch 3, dc in each st around, join with sl st in 3rd ch of beg ch-3. At end of last rnd, fasten off.

Rnd 7: Join terra-cotta with sc in first st, *sk next 2 sts, **shell** *(see Special Stitch)* in next st, sk next 2 sts**, sc in next st, rep from * around, ending last rep at **, join with sl st in beg sc. Fasten off.

Rnd 8: Join maize with sc in center dc of first shell, *shell in next sc**, sc in center dc of next shell, rep from * around, ending last rep at **, join with sl st in beg sc. Fasten off.

Rnd 9: Join taupe with sc in center dc of first shell, *shell in next sc**, sc in center dc of next shell, rep from * around, ending last rep at **, join with sl st in beg sc. Fasten off.

Rnd 10: Rep rnd 8.

Rnd 11: Join terra-cotta with sc in center dc of first shell, *shell in next sc**, sc in center dc of next shell, rep from * around, ending last rep at **, join with sl st in beg sc. Fasten off.

Rnd 12: Join lime with sc in center dc of first shell, ch 2, dc in next sc, ch 2, [sc in center dc of next shell, ch 2, dc in next sc, ch 2] around, join with sl st in beg sc. Fasten off.

Rnd 13: Join maize with sl st in first ch sp, ch 3, 2 dc in same ch sp, ch 1, [3 dc in next ch sp, ch 1] around, join with sl st in 3rd ch of beg ch-3. Fasten off.

Rnd 14: Join lime with sc in first ch sp, ch 3, [sc in next ch sp, ch 3] around, join with sl st in beg sc. Fasten off.

Rnd 15: Join taupe with sl st in first ch sp, ch 3, 2 dc in same ch sp, ch 1, [3 dc in next ch sp, ch 1] around, join with sl st in 3rd ch of beg ch-3. Fasten off.

Rnd 16: Rep rnd 14.

Rnd 17: Rep rnd 13.

Rnd 18: Rep rnd 14.

Rnd 19: Join terra-cotta with sc in first ch sp, shell in next ch sp, [sc in next ch sp, shell in next ch sp] around, join with sl st in beg sc. Fasten off.

Rnds 20–24: Rep rnds 8–12.

Rnd 25: Join taupe with sl st in ch sp at 1 side of Bag, ch 3, 2 dc in same ch sp, ch 1, [3 dc in next ch sp, ch 1] around, join with sl st in 3rd ch of beg ch-3.

Rnd 26: Ch 3, dc in each st around, join with sl st in 3rd ch of beg ch-3. Fasten off.

Rnd 27: Join lime with sc in first st, sc in each st around, join with sl st in beg sc.

Rnd 28: Working from left to right, ch 1, **reverse sc** *(see Fig. 1)* in each st around, join with sl st in beg reverse sc. Fasten off.

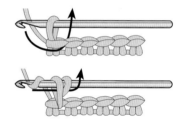

**Reverse Single Crochet
Fig. 1**

HANDLE

Row 1: With taupe, work dc foundation st 100 times.

Row 2: Ch 3, dc in each st across, turn. Fasten off.

Rnd 3: Now working in rnds, join lime with sc in first st, sc in each st across, 3 sc in end of each of next 2 rows, working in opposite side of Foundation on opposite side of row 1, sc in each st across, 3 sc in end of last 2 rows, join with sl st in beg sc.

Rnd 4: Working from left to right, ch 1, reverse sc in each st around, join with sl st in beg reverse sc. Fasten off.

With sewing needle and sewing thread, sew ends of Handle to Bag as shown in photo.

TREBLE CROCHET FOUNDATION **HOT PAD**

DESIGN BY ELIZABETH ANN WHITE

SKILL LEVEL

EASY

FINISHED SIZE
5¼ x 6 inches

MATERIALS
Elmore-Pisgah Peaches & Crème medium (worsted) weight cotton yarn (2½ oz/122 yds/71g per ball):

1 ball #21 shrimp
• Size H/8/5mm crochet hook

GAUGE
Gauge for this project is not important.

PATTERN NOTE
Chain-3 at beginning of row or round counts as first double crochet, unless otherwise stated.

FOUNDATION STITCH
Treble crochet foundation stitch (tr foundation st):
Ch 4, yo twice, insert hook in 4th ch from hook, yo, pull lp through, yo, pull through 1 lp on hook, *(base ch completed)*, [yo, pull through 2 lps on hook] 3 times;

Next st: *Yo twice, insert hook in last base ch completed, yo, pull lp through, yo, pull through 1 lp on hook, [yo, pull through 2 lps on hook] 3 times, rep from * until desired number of sts have been completed.

INSTRUCTIONS
HOT PAD
Row 1: Work **tr foundation st** *(see Foundation Stitch)* 24 times, turn.

Row 2: Ch 3 *(see Pattern Note)*, **fptr** *(see Stitch Guide)* around each of next 2 sts, [dc in each of next 2 sts, fptr around each of next 2 sts] across, ending with dc in last st, turn.

Row 3: Ch 3, **bptr** *(see Stitch Guide)* around each of next 2 sts, [dc in each of next 2 sts, bptr around each of next 2 sts] across, ending with dc in last st, turn.

Rows 4–9: [Rep rows 2 and 3 alternately] 3 times.

Row 10: Rep row 2. Fasten off. ●

TREBLE CROCHET FOUNDATION
CROWNS & LACE TABLE TOPPER

DESIGN BY SHIRLEY BROWN

SKILL LEVEL

INTERMEDIATE

FINISHED SIZE
28½ x 24 inches

MATERIALS
- Red Heart Luster Sheen fine (sport) weight yarn (4 oz/ 335 yds/113g per skein): 2 skeins #0246 peach
- Size G/6/4mm crochet hook or size needed to obtain gauge

GAUGE
4 tr = 1 inch

PATTERN NOTE
Chain-4 at beginning of row or round counts as first treble crochet, unless otherwise stated.

FOUNDATION STITCH
Treble crochet foundation stitch (tr foundation st):
Ch 4, yo twice, insert hook in 4th ch from hook, yo, pull lp through, yo, pull through 1 lp on hook, *(base ch completed)*, [yo, pull through 2 lps on hook] 3 times;

Next st: *Yo twice, insert hook in last base ch completed, yo, pull lp through, yo, pull through 1 lp on hook, [yo, pull through 2 lps on hook] 3 times, rep from * until desired number of sts have been completed.

SPECIAL STITCH
Picot shell: (Sc, ch 2, hdc in 2nd ch from hook, sc) in next ch sp.

INSTRUCTIONS
TABLE TOPPER

Row 1: Tr foundation st *(see Foundation Stitch)* 93 times, turn. *(93 tr)*

Row 2: Ch 4 *(see Pattern Note)*, tr in each of next 2 sts, *ch 4, sk next st, [sc in next st, ch 4, sk next 2 sts] 13 times, sc in next st, ch 4, sk next st, tr in each of next 3 sts, rep from * across, turn. *(3 tr groups, 30 ch sps)*

Row 3: Ch 4, tr in each of next 2 sts, *ch 5, sk next ch sp, [**picot shell** *(see Special Stitch)* in next ch sp, ch 5] 13 times, sk next ch sp, tr in each of next 3 sts, rep from * across, turn.

Row 4: Ch 4, tr in each of next 2 sts, ch 6, sk next ch sp, [picot shell in next ch sp, ch 6] 13 times, tr in each of next 3 sts, ch 6, [picot shell in next ch sp, ch 6] 13 times, sk last ch sp, tr in each of last 3 sts, turn.

Row 5: Ch 4, tr in each of next 2 sts, ch 3, [picot shell in next ch sp, ch 6] across to 1 ch sp before tr sts, sk next ch sp, tr in each of next 3 sts, ch 6, sk next ch sp, [picot shell in next ch sp, ch 6] across to 1 ch sp before last 3 sts, picot shell in last ch sp, ch 3, tr in each of last 3 sts, turn.

Row 6: Ch 4, tr in each of next 2 sts, ch 6, sk next ch sp, [picot shell in next ch sp, ch 6] across

to 1 ch sp before next tr sts, picot shell in next ch sp, ch 3, tr in each of next 3 sts, ch 3, [picot shell in next ch sp, ch 6] across to last ch sp, sk last ch sp, tr in each of last 3 sts, turn.

Rows 7–12: [Rep rows 5 and 6 alternately] 3 times.

Row 13: Rep row 5.

Row 14: Ch 1, sl st in each of next 3 sts, sk next ch sp, ch 6, [picot shell in next ch sp, ch 6] across to 1 ch sp before tr sts, picot shell in next ch sp, ch 3, sl st in each of next 3 sts, ch 3, [picot shell in next ch sp, ch 6] across to last ch sp, sk last ch sp, sl st in each of last 3 sts, turn.

Row 15: Ch 4, working over sl sts, tr in each of next 2 sts on row before last, ch 3, [picot shell in next ch sp, ch 6] across to 1 ch sp before next tr sts, sk next ch sp, working over sl sts, tr in each of next 3 sts on row before last, ch 6, sk next ch sp, [picot shell in next ch sp, ch 6] across to last ch sp, picot shell in last ch sp, ch 3, working over sl sts, tr in each of last 3 sts on row before last, turn.

Rows 16–25: [Rep rows 6 and 5 alternately] 5 times.

Row 26: Rep row 6.

Row 27: Ch 1, sl st in each of first 3 sts, ch 3, [picot shell in

next ch sp, ch 6] across to 1 ch sp before tr sts, sk next ch sp, sl st in each of next 3 sts, ch 6, sk next ch sp, [picot shell in next ch sp, ch 6] across to 1 ch sp before last 3 sts, picot shell in last ch sp, ch 3, sl st in each of last 3 sts, turn.

Row 28: Ch 4, working over sl sts, tr in each of next 2 sts on row before last, ch 6, [picot shell in next ch sp, ch 6] across to 1 ch sp before next tr sts, picot shell in next ch sp, ch 3, working over sl sts, tr in each of next 3 sts on row before last, ch 3, [picot shell in next ch sp, ch 6] across to last ch sp, sk last ch sp, working over sl sts, tr in each of last 3 sts on row before last, turn.

Rows 29–34: [Rep rows 5 and 6 alternately] 3 times.

Row 35: Rep row 5.

Row 36: Ch 1, sl st in each of first 3 sts, ch 4, sk next ch sp, [sc in next ch sp, ch 4] across to tr sts, sl st in each of next 3 sts, [ch 4, sc in next ch sp] across to last ch sp, ch 4, sk last ch sp, sl st in each of last 3 sts, turn.

Row 37: Ch 4, working over sl sts, tr in each of next 2 sts on row before last, [evenly sp 42 tr in ch sps and sts across to sl sts, working over sl sts, tr in each of next 3 sts on row before last] twice. Fasten off. ●

Chain-Free Crochet

DOUBLE CROCHET, CHAIN 1 FOUNDATION **WOVEN PLACE MAT**

DESIGN BY ELIZABETH ANN WHITE

SKILL LEVEL

INTERMEDIATE

FINISHED SIZE
14½ x 15½ inches

MATERIALS
- Elmore-Pisgah Peaches & Crème medium (worsted) weight cotton yarn (2½ oz/ 122 yds/71g per ball):
    1 ball #121 chocolate, #52 light sage and #13 burnt orange
- Size H/8/5mm crochet hook
- Fabric glue

GAUGE
4 dc and 3 ch sps = 2 inches; 4 dc rows = 2½ inches

PATTERN NOTE
Chain-4 at beginning of row or round counts as first double crochet and chain-1 space, unless otherwise stated.

FOUNDATION STITCH
Double crochet with chain-1 foundation (dc, ch-1 foundation): This will give you a foundation of dc's with ch-1 sps between them:

Ch 4, yo twice, insert hook in 4th ch from hook, yo, pull lp through, yo, pull through 2 lps on hook *(ch sp completed)*, yo, pull through 1 lp on hook *(base ch completed)*, [yo, pull through 2 lps on hook] twice *(dc completed);*

Next st: *Ch 1, yo twice, insert hook in last base ch completed, yo, pull lp through, yo, pull through 2 lps on hook, yo, pull through 1 lp on hook, [yo, pull through 2 lps on hook] twice, rep from * for desired number of sts.

INSTRUCTIONS
PLACE MAT
Row 1: With chocolate work **dc, ch-1 foundation st** *(see Foundation Stitch)* 26 times, turn. *(26 dc)*

Rows 2–5: Ch 4 *(see Pattern Note)*, dc in next dc, [ch 1, dc in next dc] across, turn. At end of last row, fasten off.

Row 6: Join light sage with sl st in first st, ch 4, dc in next dc, [ch 1, dc in next dc] across, turn.

Rows 7–10: Ch 4, dc in next dc, [ch 1, dc in next dc] across, turn. At end of last row, fasten off.

Row 11: Join chocolate with sl st in first st, ch 4, dc in next dc, [ch 1, dc in next dc] across, turn.

Rows 12–15: Ch 4, dc in next dc, [ch 1, dc in next dc] across, turn. At end of last row, fasten off.

Row 16: Join burnt orange with sl st in first st, ch 4, dc in next dc, [ch 1, dc in next dc] across, turn.

Rows 17–20: Ch 4, dc in next dc, [ch 1, dc in next dc] across, turn. At end of last row, fasten off.

Row 21: Join chocolate with sl st in first st, ch 4, dc in next dc, [ch 1, dc in next dc] across, turn.

Rows 22–25: Ch 4, dc in next dc, [ch 1, dc in next dc] across, turn. At end of last row, do not fasten off.

Rnd 26: Working around outer edge in ends of rows and on opposite side of dc with ch 1 foundation sts, ch 1, sc in each st across with 2 sc in each ch sp and 3 sc in each corner, join with sl st in beg sc. Fasten off.

WEAVING
Cut 4 strands of yarn, each 24 inches in length. Weave through ch sps of Place Mat from 1 short end to other short end.

Beg with 4 strands of chocolate, weave over and under ch sps on 1 long edge, leaving long ends for fringe on each end.

Rep 4 times with chocolate so that there are 5 rows of chocolate.

Rep with light sage so that there are 5 rows of light sage.

Rep with chocolate so that there are 5 rows of chocolate.

Rep with burnt orange so that there are 5 rows of burnt orange.

Rep with chocolate so that there are 5 rows of chocolate.

Dot glue on edges of Place Mat to hold fringe in place. ●

Chain-Free Crochet

SMALL V-STITCH FOUNDATION
POLKA DOT TEA COZY

DESIGN BY ELIZABETH ANN WHITE

SKILL LEVEL

EASY

FINISHED SIZE
7½ inches high x 21 inches around

MATERIALS
- Elmore-Pisgah Peaches & Crème medium (worsted) weight cotton yarn (2½ oz/122 yds/71g per ball):
    1 ball each #121 chocolate and #52 light sage
    1 oz/50 yds/28g #13 burnt orange
- Size H/8/5mm crochet hook
- Tapestry needle
- Fabric glue

GAUGE
3 dc = 1 inch; 2 dc rows = 1 inch

PATTERN NOTE
Chain-3 at beginning of row or round counts as first double crochet unless otherwise stated.

FOUNDATION STITCH
Small V-stitch foundation (small V-st foundation): This will give you a foundation of (dc, ch 1, dc) V-sts with a ch-2 sp between their bases;

Ch 4, dc in 4th ch from hook *(first small V-st completed)*, *yo 3 times, insert hook in same ch last V-st was worked in, yo, pull lp through, [yo, pull through 2 lps on hook] twice *(2 chs completed)*, yo, pull through 1 lp on hook *(base ch completed)*, [yo, pull through 2 lps on hook] twice, ch 1, yo, insert hook in last base ch completed, yo, pull lp through, [yo, pull through 2 lps on hook] twice *(small V-st completed)*, rep from * until desired number of sts have been completed.

INSTRUCTIONS
COZY
Rnd 1: With chocolate, leaving 6-inch end before slip knot, work **small V-st foundation** *(see Foundation Stitch)* 22 times, join with sl st in 3rd ch of beg ch-4.

Rnd 2: Sl st in ch sp of first small V-st foundation st, **ch 3** *(see Pattern Note)*, 2 dc in same ch sp, 3 dc in ch sp of each small V-st foundation st around, join with sl st in 3rd ch of beg ch-3. *(66 dc)*

FIRST SIDE

Row 3: Now working in rows, ch 3, dc in each of next 32 sts, leaving rem sts unworked, turn.

Rows 4–9: Ch 3, dc in each st across, turn. At end of last row, fasten off.

2ND SIDE

Row 3: Join chocolate with sl st in first unworked st on rnd 2, ch 3, dc in each unworked st across, turn.

Rows 4–9: Ch 3, dc in each st across, turn.

BOTH SIDES

Rnd 10: Now working in rnds, ch 3, dc in each st across 2nd Side, dc in each st across First Side, join with sl st in 3rd ch of beg ch-3. *(66 dc)*

Rnd 11: Ch 3, dc in each st around, join with sl st in 3rd ch of beg ch-3. Fasten off.

Rnd 12: Join light sage with sc in first st, working from left to right, **reverse sc** *(see Fig. 1)* in each st around, join with sl st in beg sc. Fasten off.

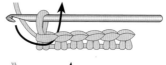
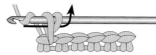

**Reverse Single Crochet
Fig. 1**

Weave 6-inch end at beg through bottom of small V-st foundation sts, pull to close. Secure end.

TOP

Rnd 1: With light sage, ch 4, 11 dc in 4th ch from hook, join with sl st in 3rd ch of beg ch-3. *(12 dc)*

Rnd 2: Ch 3, dc in same st, dc in next st, [2 dc in next st, dc in next st] around, join with sl st in 3rd ch of beg ch-3.

Rnd 3: Ch 2 *(does not count as first st)*, dc in next st, [**dc dec** *(see Stitch Guide)* in next 2 sts] around, join with sl st in top of beg dc. Fasten off.

Sew to rnd 1 of Cozy.

LARGE POLKA DOT
**Make 3 burnt orange.
Make 2 light sage.**
Ch 4, 11 dc in 4th ch from hook, join with sl st in 4th ch of beg ch-4. Fasten off.

SMALL POLKA DOT
Make 3 burnt orange and 2 light sage.
Ch 2, 6 sc in 2nd ch from hook, join with sl st in beg sc. Fasten off.

FINISHING
Glue 1 Small Polka Dot to top of Top. Glue rem Large and Small Polka Dots to 1 side of Cozy. ●

LARGE V-STITCH FOUNDATION
MOCHA LATTE SCARF

DESIGN BY ELIZABETH ANN WHITE

SKILL LEVEL

EASY

FINISHED SIZE
5¼ x 69 inches

MATERIALS
- Moda Dea Metro bulky (chunky) weight yarn (3½ oz/ 124 yds/100g per skein): 2 skeins #9863 mocha latte
- Size H/8/5mm crochet hook or size needed to obtain gauge

GAUGE
3 V-sts = 3½ inches; 7 pattern rows = 5¼ inches

PATTERN NOTE
Chain-3 at beginning of each row or round **does not** count as first double crochet throughout.

FOUNDATION STITCH
Large V-stitch foundation (large V-st foundation): This will give you a foundation of (dc, ch 2, dc) V-sts with a ch-3 sp between their bases;

Ch 5, dc in 5th ch from hook *(first large V-st completed)*, *yo 4 times, insert hook in same ch last large V-st was worked in, yo, pull lp through, [yo, pull through 2 lps on hook] 3 times *(3 chs completed)*, yo, pull through 1 lp on hook *(base ch completed)*, [yo, pull through 2 lps on hook] twice, ch 2, yo, insert hook in last base ch completed, yo, pull lp through, [yo, pull through 2 lps on hook] twice, rep from * until desired number of sts have been completed.

SPECIAL STITCHES
Shell: (2 dc, ch 2, 2 dc) in st or ch sp as indicated.
V-stitch (V-st): (Dc, ch 2, dc) as indicated.

INSTRUCTIONS
SCARF
Row 1: Work **large V-st foundation** *(see Foundation Stitch)* 59 times, turn.

Row 2: Ch 3 *(see Pattern Note)*, **shell** *(see Special Stitches)* in ch sp of first large V-st, [dc in ch sp of next V-st, shell in ch sp of next large V-st] across, turn.

Row 3: Ch 3, **V-st** *(see Special Stitches)* in ch sp of first shell, [V-st in next dc between shells, V-st in ch sp of next shell] across, turn.

Rows 4–7: [Rep rows 2 and 3 alternately] twice. At end of last row, fasten off. ●

OPEN SHELL FOUNDATION
VICTORIAN BABY CAPE

DESIGN BY ELIZABETH ANN WHITE

SKILL LEVEL

EASY

FINISHED SIZE
Infants 6 to 12 months

MATERIALS
- Caron Simply Soft medium (worsted) weight yarn (6 oz/330 yds/170g per skein):
  3 skeins #9702 off-white
- Size H/8/5mm crochet hook or size needed to obtain gauge
- Sewing needle
- Off-white sewing thread 2-inch-wide cream satin ribbon: 2 yds

GAUGE
2 shells and 1 ch-1 sp = 3 inches; 3 shell rows = 2 inches

Take time to check gauge.

PATTERN NOTES
Open shell foundation will give you a row of shells with a chain-3 space between bottom of stitches.

Chain-3 at beginning of row or round counts as first double crochet unless otherwise stated.

FOUNDATION STITCH
Open shell foundation: This will give you a foundation of (2 dc, ch 2, 2 dc) shells with a ch-3 sp between their bases;

Ch 4, (dc, ch 2, 2 dc) in 4th ch from hook, *yo 4 times, insert hook in same ch last shell was worked in, yo, pull lp through, [yo, pull through 2 lps on hook] 3 times *(3 chs completed)*, yo, pull through 1 lp on hook *(base ch completed)*, [yo, pull through 2 lps on hook] twice, (dc, ch 2, 2 dc) in last base ch completed, rep from * until desired number of sts have been completed.

SPECIAL STITCHES
Shell: (2 dc, ch 2, 2 dc) in st or sp as indicated.
Double crochet eyelet (dc eyelet): Ch 3, dc in 3rd ch from hook.

INSTRUCTIONS
CAPE
BODY
Row 1: Work **open shell foundation** *(see Foundation Stitch)* 24 times, turn. *(24 shells)*

Rows 2–42: Ch 3 *(see Pattern Note)*, [**shell** *(see Special Stitches)* in ch sp of next shell, ch 1] across, ending with shell in ch sp of last shell, turn. At end of last row, fasten off.

HOOD
Row 1: Work **dc eyelet** *(see Special Stitches)* 7 times, working in ch sp on 1 side of dc eyelet, (sl st, ch 3—*counts as dc*, dc, ch 2, 2 dc) in first ch sp, shell in each of next 5 ch sps, 2 shell in last ch sp, working on opposite side of dc eyelet, shell in each sp across, turn.

Rows 2–10: Ch 3, shell in ch sp of each shell across, ending with dc in last st of last shell, turn. At end of last row, fasten off.

FINISHING
Run gathering thread along row 1 edge of Body. Gather to fit ends of rows on Hood.

Sew Hood to gathered edge of Body.

Weave ribbon through sps of row 1 on Body. Trim ends of ribbon in a V-notch as shown in photo. ●

SOLID SHELL FOUNDATION
RIPPLING SHELLS AFGHAN

DESIGN BY ELIZABETH ANN WHITE

SKILL LEVEL

EASY

FINISHED SIZE

46 x 60 inches

MATERIALS

- Red Heart Soft Yarn medium (worsted) weight (5 oz/256 yds/140g per skein): 6 skeins each #9344 chocolate and #9518 teal
- Size H/8/5mm crochet hook or size needed to obtain gauge

GAUGE

3 sc and 2 shells = 4½ inches; 3 rows = 2 inches

PATTERN NOTE

Chain-3 at beginning of row or round counts as first double crochet, unless otherwise stated.

FOUNDATION STITCH

Solid shell foundation: This will give you a foundation of alternating sc and 5 dc shells with ch-2 sps between their bases; ch 2, insert hook in 2nd ch from hook, yo, pull lp through, yo, pull through 1 lp on hook *(base ch completed)*, yo,

pull through 2 lps on hook *(sc completed)*, *yo 3 times, insert hook in last base sc completed, yo, pull lp through, [yo, pull through 2 lps on hook] twice, yo, pull through 1 lp on hook *(base ch completed)*, [yo, pull through 2 lps on hook] twice *(dc completed)*, work 4 more dc in last base ch completed, yo twice, insert hook in last base ch completed, yo, pull lp through, [yo, pull through 2 lps on hook] twice, yo, pull through 1 lp on hook *(base ch completed)*, yo, pull through 2 lps on hook *(sc completed)*, rep from * until desired number of sts have been completed.

SPECIAL STITCH

Shell: 5 dc in st or ch sp as indicated

INSTRUCTIONS
AFGHAN

Row 1: With teal work **solid shell foundation** *(see Foundation Stitch)* 25 times, turn. *(25 shells, 26 sc)*

Row 2: Ch 3 *(see Pattern Note)*, 2 dc in same st, sc in center dc of next shell, [**shell** *(see Special Stitch)* in next sc, sc in center dc of next shell] across, ending with 3 dc in last sc, turn. Fasten off.

Row 3: Join chocolate with sc in first st, shell in next sc, [sc in center dc of next shell, shell in next sc] across, ending with sc in last st, turn.

Row 4: Ch 3, 2 dc in same st, sc in center dc of next shell, [shell in next sc, sc in center dc of next shell] across, ending with 3 dc in last st. Fasten off.

Next rows: Rep rows 3 and 4 alternately and alternating colors until Afghan measures 60 inches. At end of last row, fasten off. ●

SLIP RING FOUNDATION
DOUBLE DELIGHT PILLOW

DESIGN BY MARGRET WILSON

If you want to create rounds of crochet without an annoying hole in the center, the wonderful slip ring is just what you have been looking for! A traditional Irish crochet technique, this little ring is easy and fun to do.

SKILL LEVEL

INTERMEDIATE

FINISHED SIZE
14 inches in diameter

MATERIALS
- Red Heart Soft Yarn medium (worsted) weight (5 oz/256 yds/140g per skein): 1 skein each #9344 chocolate and #9518 teal
- Size H/8/5mm crochet hook or size needed to obtain gauge
- Fiberfill

GAUGE
Rnds 1–3 = 4 inches

PATTERN NOTE
Chain-3 at beginning of row or round counts as first double crochet, unless otherwise stated.

FOUNDATION STITCH
Slip ring: Leaving 4-inch end on yarn, lap yarn over 4-inch end forming lp, insert hook through lp from front to back, yo (see step

1 of Fig. 1), pull through lp to form ring, yo, pull through lp on hook (see step 2 of Fig. 1).

Step 1

4" End

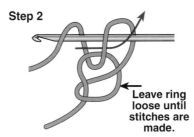

Step 2

Leave ring loose until stitches are made.

Slip Ring Foundation Stitch Fig. 1

SPECIAL STITCHES
Popcorn (pc): 4 dc in next st, drop lp from hook, insert hook in first dc of group, pull dropped lp through, ch 1.
Front post double crochet decrease (fpdc dec): Holding back last lp of each st on hook, fpdc around each of next 2 sts, yo, pull through all lps on hook.

INSTRUCTIONS
PILLOW
SIDE
Make 1 with teal.
Make 1 with chocolate.
Rnd 1: Make **slip ring** (see Foundation Stitch), **ch 3** (see Pattern Note), 15 dc in ring, join with sl st in 3rd ch of beg ch-3. Pull end of yarn to close ring.

Rnd 2: Sl st in next sp between sts, ch 3, **fpdc** (see Stitch Guide) around next st, [dc in next sp between sts, fpdc around next dc] around, join with sl st in 3rd ch of beg ch-3. (32 sts)

Rnd 3: Ch 3, dc in same st, fpdc around next st, [2 dc in next dc, fpdc around next st] around, join with sl st in 3rd ch of beg ch-3. (48 sts)

Rnd 4: Ch 3, dc in next sp between sts, dc in next dc, fpdc around next st, [dc in next dc, dc in next sp between sts, dc in next dc, fpdc around next st] around, join with sl st in 3rd ch of beg ch-3. (64 sts)

Rnd 5: Ch 3, **pc** (see Special Stitches) in next dc, dc in next dc, fpdc around next st, [dc in next dc, pc in next dc, dc in next dc, fpdc around next st] around, join with sl st in 3rd ch of beg ch-3.

Rnd 6: Ch 3, fpdc around last post st made, fpdc around next pc, [sk next dc, fpdc around

next post st, dc in sk dc behind post st just made, dc in next dc, working in front of last dc made, fpdc around same post st as last fpdc made, fpdc around next pc] 15 times, sk next dc, fpdc around same post st as first fpdc made, dc in sk dc behind fpdc just made, join with sl st in 3rd ch of beg ch-3.

Rnd 7: Ch 3, *sk next fpdc, dc in next fpdc, **fpdc dec** (see Special Stitches), dc in same st as last dc made, dc in next dc, dc in next sp between sts**, dc in next dc, rep from * around, ending last rep at **, join with sl st in 3rd ch of beg ch-3.

Rnd 8: Ch 3, dc in next dc, *fpdc around next dec post st, dc in each of next 2 dc, pc in next dc**, dc in each of next 2 dc, rep from * around, ending last rep at **, join with sl st in 3rd ch of beg ch-3.

Rnd 9: Ch 3, sk next dc, *fpdc around next post st, dc in sk st behind post st just made, dc in next dc, fpdc around same post st as last fpdc made, dc in next dc, fpdc around next pc**, dc in next dc, sk next dc, rep from * around, ending last rep at **, join with sl st in 3rd ch of beg ch-3.

Rnd 10: Ch 3, *dc in next dc, dc in next sp between sts, dc in each of next 2 dc, fpdc around next post st, dc in next dc**, sk next dc, fpdc around next post st, dc in sk dc behind post st just made, rep from * around, ending last rep at **, join with sl st in 3rd ch of beg ch-3.

Rnd 11: Ch 3, dc in next dc, *pc in next dc, dc in each of next 3 dc, fpdc dec, dc in same st as last dc made**, dc in each of next 2 dc, rep from * around, ending last rep at **, join with sl st in 3rd ch of beg ch-3.

Rnd 12: Ch 3, dc in next dc, *fpdc around next pc, dc in each of next 3 dc, fpdc around next fpdc dec**, dc in each of next 3 dc, rep from * around, ending last rep at **, join with sl st in 3rd ch of beg ch-3.

Rnd 13: Ch 3, dc in same st, dc in next dc, [fpdc around next post st, dc in next dc, 2 dc in next dc, dc in next dc] 31 times, fpdc around next post st, dc in last dc, join with sl st in 3rd ch of beg ch-3.

For **First Side**, fasten off.

For **2nd Side**, do not fasten off.

Rnd 14: Holding both Side pieces WS tog, working through both thicknesses, stuffing with fiberfill before closing, sl st in each st around, join with sl st in beg sl st. Fasten off. ●

ROLLED RING FOUNDATION
SAND PEBBLES TABLE RUNNER

Design by Shirley Brown

If you want an open ring instead of closed one, try this clever technique! Wrapping the yarn around your fingers several times and then working a round of single crochet over the strands is also a traditional Irish crochet method for starting motifs.

SKILL LEVEL

INTERMEDIATE

FINISHED SIZE
20 x 48 inches

MATERIALS
- Red Heart LusterSheen fine (sport) weight yarn (4 oz/335 yds/113g per skein):
  2 skeins #0332 tan
- Size D/3/3.25mm crochet hook or size needed to obtain gauge

GAUGE
3 eyelet cls = 2 inches

PATTERN NOTE
Cannot give size of each Motif because this depends on how large the center is.

FOUNDATION STITCH
Rolled ring: Wrap yarn several times around 1 or more fingers to adjust size of center. Slide yarn off finger or fingers, sl st or sc in ring. Complete according to instructions.

SPECIAL STITCHES
Double crochet eyelet cluster (dc eyelet cl): Ch 3, dc in 3rd ch from hook.
Joining: Ch 3, sl st in corresponding ch-7 sp on other Motif, ch 3, sl st in first ch of beg ch-3.

INSTRUCTIONS
RUNNER
FIRST MOTIF
Rnd 1: Rolled ring foundation *(see Foundation Stitch)* ch 1, 24 sc in circle, join with sl st in beg sc. *(24 sc)*

Rnd 2: Ch 1, sc in each of first 2 sts, *ch 2, **dc dec** (see Stitch Guide) in last st worked in and next st, ch 2, sc in same st**, sc in each of next 2 sts, rep from * around, ending last rep at **, join with sl st in beg sc.

Rnd 3: Ch 1, sc in first st, *2 **dc eyelet cls** (see Special Stitches), sc in top of dc dec, 2 eyelet cls, ch 1, sk next sc**, sc in next sc, rep from * around, ending last rep at **, join with sl st in beg sc.

Rnd 4: Ch 1, sc in first st, *ch 10, sl st in 3rd ch from hook, ch 7, sl st in 7th ch from hook, ch 3, sl st in 3rd ch from hook, ch 7, sk next sc**, sc in next sc, rep from * around, ending last rep at **, join with sl st in beg sc. Fasten off.

2ND MOTIF
Rnds 1–3: Rep rnds 1–3 of First Motif.

Rnd 4: Ch 1, sc in first st, [ch 10, sl st in 3rd ch from hook, ch 7, sl st in 7th ch from hook, ch 3, sl st in 3rd ch from hook, ch 7, sk next sc, sc in next sc] 6 times, ch 10, sl st in 3rd ch from hook, **joining** *(see Special Stitches)*, ch 3, sl st in 3rd ch from hook, ch 7, sk next sc, sc in next sc, ch 10, sl st in 3rd ch from hook, joining,

ch 3, sl st in 3rd ch from hook, ch 7, sk next sc, join with sl st in beg sc. Fasten off.

3RD MOTIF

Rnds 1–3: Rep rnds 1–3 of First Motif.

Rnd 4: Ch 1, sc in first st, [ch 10, sl st in 3rd ch from hook, ch 7, sl st in 7th ch from hook, ch 3, sl st in 3rd ch from hook, ch 7, sk next sc, sc in next sc] 4 times, [ch 10, sl st in 3rd ch from hook, joining, ch 3, sl st in 3rd ch from hook, ch 7, sk next sc, sc in next sc] 3 times, ch 10, sl st in 3rd ch from hook, joining, ch 3, sl st in 3rd ch from hook, ch 7, join with sl st in beg sc. Fasten off.

Working 2nd and 3rd Motifs as needed to join, make 7 rows of 3 Motifs.

BORDER

Rnd 1: Beg at corner before 1 long edge, join with sl st in ch-7 sp, *[3 dc eyelet cl, sl st in next ch-7 sp, 3 dc eyelet cl, sl st in joining between Motifs, 3 dc eyelet cls, sl st in next ch-7 sp] across to corner, 3 dc eyelet cls, sl st in next ch-7 sp, 4 dc eyelet cls at corner**, sl st in next ch-7 sp, rep from * around, ending last rep at **, join with sl st in beg sl st.

Rnd 2: Ch 5, sl st in 5th ch from hook, *[ch 5, sl st in 2nd eyelet, ch 5, sl st in 5th ch from hook, ch 5, sl st in next sl st, ch 5, sl st in 5th ch from hook] across to corner, sl st between 2nd and 3rd dc eyelet cls at corner, ch 5, sl st in 5th ch from hook, rep from * around, join with sl st in beg sl st. Fasten off.

Block to measurement. ●

DOUBLE CROCHET EYELET FOUNDATION CORAL BELLS CANDLE MAT

DESIGN BY ELIZABETH ANN WHITE

When you need a row or round of chain spaces to begin your project, the eyelet foundations can't be beat.

SKILL LEVEL

INTERMEDIATE

FINISHED SIZE
12½ inches in diameter

MATERIALS
Size 10 crochet cotton:
    200 yds ecru
    150 yds coral
    100 yds light green
Size 7/1.65mm steel crochet hook or size needed to obtain gauge

GAUGE
Rnd 1 = 4½ inches in diameter before center trim

PATTERN NOTES
Chain-4 at beginning of row or round counts as first double crochet and chain-1 unless otherwise stated.

Chain-7 at beginning of row or round counts as first treble crochet and chain-3 unless otherwise stated.

5 petals make up flower, 3 petals form outer edge of Mat.

Wrong side of stitches on petals will face out on all flowers.

FOUNDATION STITCH
Double crochet eyelet (dc eyelet): [Ch 3, dc in 3rd ch from hook] number of times stated.

INSTRUCTIONS
CANDLE MAT

Rnd 1: Work **dc eyelet foundation** *(see Foundation Stitch)* 32 times, join with sl st in first ch of beg dc eyelet foundation to form ring, (sc, ch 4, sc, ch 4) in each ch sp around, join with sl st in beg sc.

Rnds 2–12: Sl st to center of first ch sp, ch 1, sc in first ch sp, ch 4, [sc in next ch sp, ch 4] around, join with sl st in beg sc. At end of last rnd, fasten off.

Rnd 13: Join light green with sl st in first ch sp, **ch 4** *(see Pattern Notes)*, (dc, ch 1, dc, ch 1) in same ch sp, (dc, ch 1) 3 times in each ch sp around, join with sl st in 3rd ch of beg ch-4.

Rnd 14: Ch 7 *(see Pattern Notes)*, [tr in next st, ch 3] around, join with sl st in 4th ch of beg ch-7. Fasten off.

Rnd 15: Join coral with sc in first ch sp, (ch 1, 5 dc, ch 1, sc) in same ch sp, (sc, ch 1, 5 dc, ch 1, sc) in each of next 7 ch sps *(8 petals completed)*, remove lp from hook, insert hook between 3rd and 4th petals, pull dropped lp through, ch 1 *(flower completed, see Pattern Notes)*, [(sc, ch 1, 5 dc, ch 1, sc) in each of next 8 ch sps, remove lp from hook, insert hook between 3rd and 4th petals, pull dropped lp through, ch 1] around, join with sl st in beg sc. Fasten off.

CENTER TRIM

Working on opposite side of dc eyelet foundation of rnd 1 on inside, join light green with sc in any sp, (ch 3, sc, ch 3) in same ch sp, (sc, ch 3, sc, ch 3) in each ch sp around, join with sl st in beg sc. Fasten off.

Block with spray starch if desired. ●

TREBLE CROCHET EYELET
FOUNDATION **BOHO BELT**

DESIGN BY ELIZABETH ANN WHITE

EASY

FINISHED SIZE

34½ inches long, excluding ties

MATERIALS

• Pepperell Braiding Co. Amy
  Cord 2mm nylon cord:
  2 skeins each meadow and
  #04 brown
• Size H/8/5mm crochet
  hook or size needed to
  obtain gauge

GAUGE

Each tr eyelet foundation st =
1½ inches

PATTERN NOTE

Chain-3 at beginning of row
or round counts as first double
crochet, unless otherwise stated.

FOUNDATION STITCH

**Treble crochet eyelet
(tr eyelet):** [Ch 4, tr in
4th ch from hook] number
of times stated.

SPECIAL STITCH

Shell: (2 dc, ch 2, 2 dc) in
st or ch sp indicated.

INSTRUCTIONS
BELT

Row 1: With brown, work **tr
eyelet foundation** (see Special
Stitches) 23 times, do not turn.
Fasten off.

Rnd 2: Now working in rnds,
join light green with sl st in
first sp, **ch 3** (see Pattern Note),
(dc, ch 2, 2 dc, ch 3, 2 dc, ch
2, 2 dc) in same sp, ch 1, sc in
next sp, ch 1, [**shell** (see Special
Stitches), in next sp, ch 1, sc in
next sp, ch 1] around to last sp,
(shell, ch 3, shell) in last sp, ch
1, working on opposite side of tr
eyelet foundation, sc in next sp,
[shell in next sp, sc in next sp]
around, join with sl st in 3rd ch
of beg ch-3. Fasten off.

Rnd 3: Join brown with sc in 1
end ch sp, ch 3, sc in same ch
sp, ch 2, (sc, ch 2, sc) in ch sp of

next shell, ch 2, sc in next ch sp,
[sc in next ch sp, ch 2, (sc, ch 2,
sc) in ch sp of next shell, ch 2,
sc in next ch sp] 10 times, sc in
next ch sp, ch 2, (sc, ch 2, sc) in
ch sp of next shell, ch 2, (sc, ch
3, sc) in ch sp at end, ch 2, (sc,
ch 2, sc) in ch sp of next shell,
ch 2, sc in next ch sp, [sc in next
ch sp, ch 2, (sc, ch 2, sc) in ch sp
of next shell, ch 2, sc in next ch
sp] 10 times, sc in next ch sp, ch
2, (sc, ch 2, sc) in ch sp of next
shell, ch 2, join with sl st in beg
sc. Fasten off.

TIE

Cut 5 strands of brown each
34 inches in length. Holding
all strands tog, fold in half. Pull
fold through sp at 1 end of Belt,
pull all ends through fold. Pull
to tighten.

Rep on other end of Belt. ●

LOVE KNOT FOUNDATION
CHOCOLATE KISSES WRAP

DESIGN BY ELIZABETH ANN WHITE

SKILL LEVEL

EASY

FINISHED SIZE
17 x 90 inches, excluding Fringe

MATERIALS
- Red Heart LusterSheen fine (sport) weight yarn (4 oz/335 yds/113g per skein):
    3 skeins #0360 chocolate
- Size F/5/3.75mm crochet hook

GAUGE
Gauge for this project is not important.

FOUNDATION STITCH
Love knot: Pull up 1-inch long lp on hook *(see Fig. 1)*, yo, pull through lp, sc in back strand of long lp.

SPECIAL STITCH
Double love knot: [Pull up 1-inch long lp on hook *(see Fig. 2)*, yo, pull through lp, sc in back strand of long lp] twice.

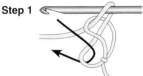
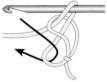
Step 1

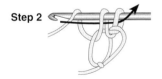
Step 2

Completed Love Knot

Step 3

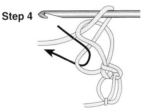
Step 4

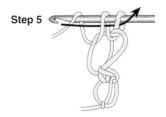
Step 5

Completed Double Love Knot

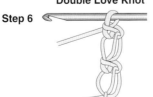
Step 6

**Love Knot Illustrations
Fig. 1**

INSTRUCTIONS
WRAP
Row 1: Ch 2, sc in 2nd ch from hook, **love knot** *(see Foundation Stitch)* 49 times.

Row 2: Sc in 5th sc from hook, [**double love knot** *(see Special Stitch)* sk next 2 love knots, sc in next sc] across, turn. *(23 double love knots)*

Row 3: 3 love knots, sc in center of first double love knot, [double love knot, sc in center of next double love knot] across, turn.

Next rows: Rep row 3 until piece measures 90 inches long. At end of last row, fasten off.

FRINGE
Cut 4 strands, each 14 inches in length. Holding all strands tog, fold in half, pull fold through, pull ends through fold. Pull to tighten.

Attach Fringe at end of each row, across 1 long side of Wrap. ●

BENDY'S SLINGSHOT CAST ON SINGLE CROCHET FOUNDATION
ALL KNIT-LOOK SWEATER

DESIGN BY BELINDA "BENDY" CARTER

SKILL LEVEL

INTERMEDIATE

FINISHED SIZES
Instructions given fit women's small; changes for medium, large and X-large are in [ ].

FINISHED GARMENT MEASUREMENTS
Bust: 40 inches *(small)* [44 inches *(medium)*, 48 inches *(large)*, 52 inches *(X-large)*]

MATERIALS
- Lion Brand Cotton-Ease medium (worsted) weight yarn (3½ oz/207 yds/ 100g per skein): 7 [8, 9, 9] skeins #122 taupe
- Sizes I/9/5.5mm and K/10½/6.5mm crochet hooks or size needed to obtain gauge
- Tapestry needle

GAUGE
Size K hook: 18 pattern sts = 5 inches; 24 pattern rows = 5 inches

Take time to check gauge.

FOUNDATION STITCH
Bendy's Slingshot Cast On Knit: Holding end in front of hook and skein in back of hook, wrapping yarn around finger using slingshot cast on *(see Fig. 1)*, slide lp off finger onto hook, *(cast on 1 st)*, yo from skein

going from back over hook and to back again, pull through both lps on hook, 1 st completed.

SPECIAL STITCH
Reverse slip stitch (reverse sl st): Working from left to right, insert hook in next st to right, yo, pull lp through st and lp on hook.

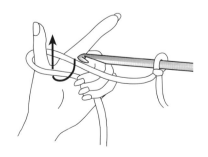

**Slingshot Cast On
Fig. 1**

INSTRUCTIONS
SWEATER
BACK
BODY
Row 1 (RS): Working from side to side, with size K hook, place slip knot on hook leaving 58-inch end at beg, work **Bendy's Slingshot Cast On Knit** *(see Foundation Stitch)* 57 times, **do not turn.** *(57 slingshot cast on sc sts)*

Row 2 (RS): Ch 1, **reverse sl st** *(see Special Stitch)* in **back lp** *(see Stitch Guide)* in each st across, do not turn.

Row 3: Ch 1, sl st in back lp of each st across, do not turn.

Rows 4–95 [4–103, 4–113, 4–123]: [Rep rows 2 and 3 alternately] 46 [50, 55, 60] times.

Row 96 [104, 114, 124]: Rep row 2.

BODICE
Row 1: Working in ends of rows with WS facing, ch 1, evenly sp 72 [79, 87, 94] sl sts across, do not turn.

Row 2 (WS): Ch 1, reverse sl st in back lp of each st across, do not turn.

ARMHOLE SHAPING
Next rows: Continue in same established pattern as on Body and at same time leave 7 sts unworked at end of each of next 2 rows. *(58 [65, 73, 80] sts at end of last row)*

Next rows: Continue working even in established pattern until piece measures 7½ [8, 8½, 8½] inches from beg of Armhole Shaping, ending with sl st row.

Be sure to measure in upright position as if being worn.

FIRST NECK SHAPING
Row 1: Ch 1, reverse sl st in back lp of each of first 17 [20, 23, 26] sts, leaving rem sts unworked, do not turn.

Row 2: Ch 1, sl st in back lp of each st across. Fasten off.

2ND NECK SHAPING
Row 1: Sk next 24 [25, 27, 28] sts, join with sl st in next st, reverse sl st in back lp of each st across, do not turn. *(17 [20, 23, 26] sl sts)*

Row 2: Ch 1, sl st in back lp of each st across. Fasten off.

FRONT
Work same as Back until Front is 10 [10, 12, 12] rows less than Back, ending with sl st row.

FIRST NECK SHAPING
Row 1: Ch 1, reverse sl st in back lp of each of first 23 [26, 31, 34] sts, leaving rem sts unworked, do not turn.

Row 2: Ch 1, sl st in back lp of each st across, do not turn.

Next rows: Continue working in established pattern and at same time leave last 2 sts unworked at end of next row at neck edge, then leave 2 sts unworked at end of every other row at neck edge 2 [2, 3, 3] times. *(17 [20, 23, 26] sl sts at end of last row)*

Next rows: Continue working even in established pattern until Front is the same as Back. At end of last row, fasten off.

2ND NECK SHAPING
Row 1: Sk next 12 [13, 11, 12] sts, join with sl st in next st, reverse sl st in back lp of each st across, do not turn. *(23 [26, 31, 34] reverse sl sts)*

Next rows: Continue working in established pattern and at same time leave last 2 sts unworked at end of next row at neck edge, then leave 2 sts

unworked at end of every other row at neck edge 2 [2, 3, 3] times. *(17 [20, 23, 26] sl sts at end of last row)*

Next rows: Continue working even in established pattern until Front is the same as Back. At end of last row, fasten off.

SLEEVE
Make 2.
PART 1
Row 1 (RS): Working from side to side, with size K hook, place slip knot on hook leaving 70-inch end at beg, work Bendy's slingshot cast on 72 times, do not turn.

Row 2: Ch 1, reverse sl st in back lp of each st across, do not turn.

Row 3: Ch 1, sl st in back lp of each st across, do not turn.

PART 1 SHAPING
Next rows: Continue in established pattern and at same time leave 5 sts unworked at end of next row at cuff edge, then leave 5 sts unworked at end of every other row at cuff edge 10 [11, 11, 11] times. At end of last row, fasten off. *(17 [12, 12, 12] sts at end of last row)*

PART 2
Row 1 (RS): With RS facing, join with sl st at sleeve shoulder edge, ch 1, evenly sp 72 reverse sl sts across, do not turn.

Row 2: Ch 1, sl st in each st across, do not turn.

Rows 3–18 [3–18, 3–20, 3–20]: Work in established pattern across, ending with sl st row.

PART 2 SHAPING
Rep Part 1 Shaping.

ASSEMBLY
Sew shoulder seams.

Fold 1 Sleeve in half lengthwise, place fold at shoulder seam, sew in place.

Rep with rem Sleeve.

Sew side and Sleeve seams.

EDGING
Rnd 1: With size I hook, join with sc in seam, evenly sp an even number of sc around, join with sl st in beg sc.

Rnd 2: Ch 1, **fpsc** *(see Stitch Guide)* around first st, **bpsc** *(see Stitch Guide)* around next st, [fpsc around next st, bpsc around next st] around, join with sl st in beg fpsc. Fasten off.

Work Edging around Neck opening, bottom edge and around each Sleeve. ●

SINGLE CROCHET TWIST FOUNDATION
BREEZY TWIST SWEATER

DESIGN BY BELINDA "BENDY" CARTER

SKILL LEVEL

INTERMEDIATE

FINISHED SIZES
Instructions given fit women's small; changes for medium, large, X-large, 2X-large and 3X-large are in [ ].

FINISHED GARMENT MEASUREMENTS
Bust: 35½ inches *(small)* [40 inches *(medium)*, 44½ inches *(large)*, 48½ inches *(X-large)*, 53 inches *(2X-large)*, 57½ inches *(3X-large)*]

MATERIALS
• Lion Brand Wool-Ease medium (worsted) weight yarn (3 oz/197 yds/85g per skein):
  6 [7, 8, 9, 10, 10] skeins #174 avocado

• Sizes H/8/5mm and J/10/6mm crochet hooks or size needed to obtain gauge
• Tapestry needle

GAUGE
Size H hook: 11 pattern sts = 4 inches; 22 pattern rows = 7 inches

Take time to check gauge.

FOUNDATION STITCH
Single crochet twist foundation (sc twist foundation): Ch 2, sc in 2nd ch from hook, turn, ch 1, sc in last sc made.

SPECIAL STITCH
Single crochet twist (sc twist): Insert hook in **front lp** *(see Stitch Guide)* of st, yo, pull lp through, insert hook in **back lp** *(see Stitch Guide)* of same st, yo, pull lp through, yo, pull through all lps on hook

INSTRUCTIONS
SWEATER
BACK
BREEZY TWIST
Make 2.
Row 1: With size J hook, ch 2, sc in 2nd ch from hook, turn. *(1 sc)*

Rows 2–49 [2–55, 2–61, 2–67, 2–73, 2–79]: Ch 1, sc in sc, turn. At end of last row, do not turn.

Row 50 [56, 62, 68, 74, 80]: Working in ends of rows, ch 1, sc in each row across. Fasten off. *(49 [55, 61, 67, 73, 79] sc)*

BODY
Row 1: Holding both Breezy Twist pieces tog, with size H hook, join with sc through both thicknesses in first st, working in front strip only, *sc in each of next 5 sts, leave 5 sts in back strip unworked, bring back strip down and back up in front of other strip, sc through both thicknesses in next st**, working in strip now in front only, rep from * across, ending last rep at **, turn. *(49 [55, 61, 67, 73, 79] sc)*

Row 2: Ch 1, sc in first st, [**sc twist** in next st, sc in next st] across, turn.

Row 3: Ch 1, sc in each of first 2 sts, [sc twist in next st, sc in next st] across, ending with sc in last st, turn.

Next rows: Rep rows 2 and 3 alternately until piece measures 14 [14½, 15, 15½, 16, 16½] inches from beg.

ARMHOLE SHAPING

Next row: Sl st in each of first 3 [4, 4, 5, 5, 6] sts, ch 1, sc in same st, work in established pattern across, leaving last 2 [3, 3, 4, 4, 5] sts unworked, turn. *(45 [49, 55, 59, 65, 69] sts)*

Next rows: Continue working in established pattern and at same time, dec 1 [1, 1, 1, 2, 2] sts on each end of next 5 [5, 6, 7, 5, 6] rows. *(35 [39, 43, 45, 45, 45] sts at end of ast row)*

Next rows: Continue working even in established pattern until piece measures 7 [7½, 7¾, 7¾, 8, 8¼] inches from beg of Armhole Shaping.

FIRST NECK SHAPING

Row 1: Ch 1, work in established pattern in first 7 [9, 10, 10, 10, 10] sts, leaving rem sts unworked, turn.

Row 2: Ch 1, work in established pattern across. Fasten off.

2ND NECK SHAPING

Row 1: Sk next 21 [21, 23, 25, 25, 25] sts on last row of Armhole Shaping, join with sc in next st, work in established pattern across, turn. *(7 [9, 10, 10, 10, 10] sc)*

Row 2: Ch 1, work in established pattern across. Fasten off.

FRONT

Work same as for Back until Front is 12 [12, 12, 14, 14, 14] rows less than Back.

FIRST NECK SHAPING

Next row: Ch 1, continue in established pattern across first 13 [15, 16, 17, 17, 17] sts, leaving rem sts unworked, turn.

Next rows: Continue in pattern at the same time, dec 1 st at neck edge on each of next 6 [6, 6, 7, 7, 7] rows. *(7 [9, 10, 10, 10, 10] sts at end of last row)*

Next rows: Continue working even in established pattern until piece measures same as Back. At end of last row, fasten off.

2ND NECK SHAPING

Next row: Sk next 9 [9, 11, 11, 11, 11] sts on last row of Armhole Shaping, join with sc in next st, work in established pattern across, turn. *(13 [15, 16, 17, 17, 17] sc)*

Next rows: Continue in pattern at the same time, dec 1 st at neck edge on each of next 6 [6, 6, 7, 7, 7] rows. *(7 [9, 10, 10, 10, 10] sts at end of last row)*

Next rows: Continue working even in established pattern until piece measures same as Back. At end of last row, fasten off.

SLEEVE
Make 2.
BREEZY TWIST
Make 2.
Row 1: Ch 2, sc in 2nd ch from hook, turn. *(1 sc)*

Rows 2–25 [2–25, 2–25, 2–31, 2–31, 2–31]: Ch 1, sc in sc, turn. At end of last row, **do not turn.**

Row 26 [26, 26, 32, 32, 32]: Working in ends of rows, ch 1, sc in each row across. Fasten off. *(25 [25, 25, 31, 31, 31] sc)*

BODY

Row 1: Holding both Breezy Twist pieces tog, join with sc through both thicknesses in first st, working in front strip only, *sc in each of next 5 sts, leave 5 sts in back strip unworked, bring back strip down and back up in front of other strip, sc through both thicknesses in next st**, working in strip now in front only, rep from * across, ending last rep at **, turn. *(25 [25, 25, 31, 31, 31] sc)*

Row 2: Ch 1, sc in first st, [sc twist in next st, sc in next st] across, turn.

Row 3: Ch 1, sc in each of first 2 sts, [sc twist in next st, sc in next st] across, ending with sc in last st, turn.

Row 4: Ch 1, 2 sc in first st, [sc twist in next st, sc in next st]

across, ending with 2 sc in last st, turn.

Next rows: Continue working in established pattern and at same time inc 1 st on each end of every 7th [5th, 4th, 5th, 3rd, 3rd] row 4 [6, 8, 6, 9, 10] times in same manner as row 4. *(35 [39, 43, 45, 51, 53] sts at end of last row)*

Next rows: Continue working even in established pattern until 17 [17, 17½, 17½, 18, 18] inches from beg.

CAP SHAPING

Next row: Sl st in each of first 3 [4, 4, 5, 5, 5] sts, ch 1, sc in same st, work in pattern across, leaving last 2 [3, 3, 4, 4, 4] sts unworked, turn. *(31 [33, 37, 37, 43, 45] sts)*

Next rows: Continue in pattern and at same time, *dec 1 st on each end of next row, work 1 [1, 1, 1, 0, 0] row even, rep from * 2 [2, 3, 2, 5, 55] times. *(25 [27, 29, 31, 31, 33] sts at end of last row)*

Next rows: Continue working even in established pattern until 3½ inches from beg of Cap Shaping.

Next rows:
Continue in pattern and at same time, dec 2 sts on each end of next 4 [4, 4, 5, 5, 6] rows. At end of last row, fasten off. *(9 [11, 13, 11, 11, 9] sts at end of last row)*

FINISHING
Sew shoulder seams.

Fold 1 Sleeve in half lengthwise, place fold at shoulder seam and sew in place.

Rep with rem Sleeve.

Sew side and Sleeve seams.

NECK TRIM
BREEZY TWIST
Make 2.
Row 1: Ch 2, sc in 2nd ch from hook, turn. *(1 sc)*

Rows 2–60 [2–60, 2–66, 2–72, 2–72, 2–72]: Ch 1, sc in sc, turn. At end of last row, **do not turn**.

Row 61 [61, 67, 73, 73, 73]: Working in ends of rows, ch 1, sc in each row across. Fasten off. *(60 [60, 66, 72, 72, 72] sc)*

NECK
With RS facing, join with sc at shoulder seam, evenly sp 59 [59, 65, 71, 71, 17] sc around neck edge, join with sl st in beg sc. Fasten off. *(60 [60, 66, 72, 72, 72] sc)*

Holding both Breezy Twist pieces upside down tog, sew first st of both strips to first st on Neck, working in front strip only, sew each of next 5 sts to opening, leaving sts on back strip unworked, [bring back strip down and back up so that it is now in front, working in front strip only, sew each of next 6 sts to Neck, leaving sts on back strip unworked] around, bring back strip down and up so that it is now it front, sew ends of front strips tog, sew ends of back strips tog. ●

PUFF STITCH FOUNDATION
PAPRIKA PUFF SCARF

DESIGN BY BELINDA "BENDY" CARTER

SKILL LEVEL

EASY

FINISHED SIZE
4 x 58 inches, excluding Fringe

MATERIALS
• Lion Brand Wool-Ease medium (worsted) weight yarn (3 oz/197 yds/85g per skein):
    2 skeins #188 paprika
• Size J/10/6mm crochet hook or size needed to obtain gauge

4
MEDIUM

GAUGE
17 puff sts = 11 inches

PATTERN NOTE
Scarf is worked lengthwise.

FOUNDATION STITCH
Puff stitch foundation stitch (puff st foundation st): Ch 1, *pull up ½ lp, [yo, insert hook in ch, yo, pull through pulling up ½-inch lp] twice, yo pull through all lps on hook, ch 1, rep from * number of times stated.

SPECIAL STITCH
Puff stitch (puff st): Ch 1, *pull up ½ lp, [yo, insert hook in ch, yo, pull through, pulling up ½-inch lp] twice, yo pull through all lps on hook, sk next st, insert hook in next st, yo, pull through st and lp on hook creating ch.

INSTRUCTIONS
SCARF
Row 1: Work **puff st foundation st** (*see Foundation Stitch*) 90 times. (*90 puff sts*)

Row 2: Ch 1, sc in 2nd ch from hook, 2 sc in each ch across to last ch, sc in last ch, turn. (*180 sc*)

Row 3: Ch 1, **puff st** (*see Special Stitch*) across, turn. (*90 puff sts*)

Rows 4–11: [Rep rows 2 and 3 alternately] 4 times. At end of last row, fasten off.

FRINGE
Cut 2 strands, each 10 inches in length. Holding both strands tog, fold in half, pull fold through, pull ends through fold. Pull to tighten.

Attach Fringe in end of each row across both short ends. ●

BENDY'S CAST ON FOUNDATION
RUSSIAN TEA-LEAF SHELL

DESIGN BY BELINDA "BENDY" CARTER

FINISHED SIZES

Instructions given fit women's small; changes for medium, large, and X-large are in [ ].

FINISHED GARMENT MEASUREMENTS

Bust: 34 inches *(small)* [38 inches *(medium)*, 42 inches *(large)*, 46 inches *(X-large)*]

MATERIALS

- Red Heart LusterSheen fine (sport) weight yarn (4 oz/335 yds/113g per skein):
  3 [4, 4, 5] skeins #0615 tea leaf
- Sizes E/4/3.5mm and G/6/4mm crochet hooks or size needed to obtain gauge
- Tapestry needle
- Traditions round beads #20-05 Russian jade: 3 bags of 50 beads
- Waxed dental floss

GAUGE

Size G hook: 25 sts = 6 inches; 22 rows = 5 inches

Take time to check gauge.

PATTERN NOTE

To make a beading needle, cut an 8-inch piece of waxed dental floss, hold the ends of floss together forming a loop *(eye of needle)*, insert end of yarn through the loop in the dental floss so that about 3 inches of the yarn is through the loop, squeeze the ends of the dental floss together so that they stick together, forming point of needle.

FOUNDATION STITCH

Bendy's cast on: Hold end in front of hook, hold skein in back of hook, yo with end going from front over hook and back to front *(2 lps on hook)*, yo with skein going from back over hook and back to back, pull through 1 lp on hook *(2 lps on hook)*, yo with skein going from back over hook and back to back, pull through both lps on hook *(st completed)*.

SPECIAL STITCH

Bead single crochet (bead sc): Pull bead up to hook, sc, bead will appear on back side of work.

INSTRUCTIONS
SHELL
BACK

Row 1 (RS): With size G hook, place slip knot on hook leaving 52 [58, 64, 70]-inch end at beg, work **Bendy's cast on** *(see Foundation Stitch)* 71 [79, 87, 95] times, turn. *(71 [79, 87, 95] Bendy's cast-on sts)*

Row 2 (WS): Ch 1, sc in each st across, turn.

Row 3 (RS): Ch 1, sc in first st, [**sc dec** *(see Stitch Guide)* in same st as last sc and in next 2 sts, sc in last st worked in] across, sc in last st, turn.

Next rows: Rep row 3 until piece measures 13 [13, 14, 15] inches from beg.

ARMHOLE SHAPING

Next row: Sl st in each of first 5 [5, 7, 9] sts, ch 1, sc in same st, [sc dec in same st as last sc and in next 2 sts, sc in last st worked in] across, leaving last 4 [4, 6, 8] sts unworked, turn. *(63 [71, 75, 79] sts)*

Next rows: Working in established pattern at the same time, dec 1 st on each end of next 7 [9, 9, 9] rows. *(49 [53, 57, 61] sts at end of last row)*

Next rows: Continue working even in established pattern until piece measures 7 [7½, 7¾, 7¾] inches from beg of Armhole Shaping.

Row 1: Ch 1, work in pattern across first 8 [10, 10, 12] sts, leaving rem sts unworked, turn.

Row 2: Work even in pattern across. Fasten off.

2ND NECK SHAPING

Row 1: Sk next 33 [33, 37, 37] sts, join with sc in next st, work in pattern across, turn. *(8 [10, 10, 12] sts)*

Row 2: Work even in pattern across. Fasten off.

FRONT

Work same as for Back until Front is 12 [12, 14, 14] rows less than Back.

FIRST NECK SHAPING

Next row: Ch 1, continue in established pattern across first 20 [22, 24, 26] sts, turn.

Next rows: Continue working in established pattern and at same time, dec 2 sts at neck edge on each of next 6 [6, 7, 7] rows. *(8 [10, 10, 12] sts at end of last row)*

Next rows: Continue working in established pattern until Front is the same length as Back. At end of last row, fasten off.

2ND NECK SHAPING

Next row: Sk next 9 sts, join with sc in next st, work in pattern across, turn. *(20 [22, 24, 26] sts)*

Next rows: Continue working in established pattern and at same time, dec 2 sts at neck edge on each of next 6 [6, 7, 7] rows. *(8 [10, 10, 12] sts at end of last row)*

Next rows: Continue working in established pattern until Front is the same length as Back. At end of last row, fasten off.

FINISHING

Sew shoulder and side seams.

BOTTOM EDGING

With RS facing, with size E hook, join with sc in 1 side seam at bottom edge, sc in each st around, join with sl st in beg sc. Fasten off.

NECK EDGING

Rnd 1: With **beading needle** *(see Pattern Note)*, string beads onto yarn, with RS facing and size E hook, join with sc at 1 shoulder seam, evenly sp an even number of sc around, join with sl st in beg sc, **turn**.

Rnd 2: Ch 1, sc in first st, **bead sc** *(see Special Stitch)* in next st, [sc in next st, bead sc in next st] around, join with sl st in beg sc.

Rnd 3: Sl st in each st around, join with sl st in beg sl st. Fasten off.

ARMHOLE EDGING

Rnd 1: Working around 1 armhole, with RS facing and size E hook, join with sc at seam, evenly sp an even number of sc around, join with sl st in beg sc, **turn**.

Rnds 2 & 3: Rep rnds 2 and 3 of Neck Edging.

Rep on rem armhole. ●

BACK BAR SINGLE CROCHET FOUNDATION **COVER UP**

DESIGN BY BELINDA "BENDY" CARTER

FINISHED SIZES

Instructions given fit women's small; changes for medium, large, X-large, 2X-large and 3X-large are in [ ].

FINISHED GARMENT MEASUREMENT

Bust: 35½ inches *(small)* [40 inches *(medium)*, 44½ inches *(large)*, 49 inches *(X-large)*, 53½ inches *(2X-large)*, 58 inches *(3X-large)*]

MATERIALS

- Lion Brand Microspun light (light worsted) weight yarn (2½ oz/ 168 yds/70g per skein):

  4 [4, 5, 5, 6, 6] skeins #124 mocha
  Size H/8/5mm and I/9/5.5mm crochet hooks or size needed to obtain gauge
- 1-inch button
- Stitch markers

GAUGE

Size I hook: 9 sts = 5 inches; 10 pattern rows = 5 inches when piece is laying flat

Take time to check gauge.

PATTERN NOTE

When working to a certain number of inches, measure piece laying flat on table. Cover Up will be approximately 2½ inches longer when worn.

FOUNDATION STITCH

Back bar single crochet (back bar sc): Ch 1, sc in back bar of ch *(see Fig. 2)* as stated.

**Back Bar of Chain
Fig. 1**

SPECIAL STITCHES

Beginning single love knot (beg single love knot): Pull lp on hook up ⅓-inch, insert hook in sc, yo, pull through st and up even with work, yo, pull through both lps on hook, sc in back lp of st just made *(see Fig. 1)*.

Step 1

Step 2

Step 3

**Beginning Single Love Knot
Fig. 2**

Single love knot: Insert hook in sc, yo, pull through and up even with work, yo, pull through both lps on hook, sc in back lp of st just made (see Fig. 1).

Beginning single love knot decrease (beg single love knot dec): Pull lp on hook up ⅓-inch, insert hook in sc, yo, pull through and up even with work, insert hook in next sc, yo, pull through and up even with work, yo, pull through all lps on hook, sc in back lp of st just made.

Single love knot decrease (single love knot dec): Insert hook in sc, yo, pull through and up even with work, insert hook in next sc, yo, pull through and up even with work, yo, pull through all lps on hook, sc in back lp of st just made.

INSTRUCTIONS
COVER UP
BACK

Row 1: With size I hook, **back bar sc** (see Foundation Stitch) of ch] 32 [36, 40, 44, 48, 52] times, turn.

Row 2: Beg single love knot (see Special Stitches) in first st, **single love knot** (see Special Stitches) in each st across, turn.

Next rows: Rep row 2 until piece measures 12 [12, 12, 13, 13, 13] inches from beg.

ARMHOLE SHAPING

Next row: Sl st across to sp before 3rd [3rd, 4th, 4th, 4th, 4th] sc, beg single love knot, single love knot across, leaving last 2 [2, 3, 3, 3, 3] sts unworked, turn. (28 [32, 34, 38, 42, 46] sts)

Next rows: Continued in pattern and at same time using **beg single love knot dec** (see Special Stitches) and **single love knot dec** (see Special Stitches), dec 1 [1, 1, 1, 2, 2] sts at each end of next row, dec 0 [0, 0, 1, 1, 2] sts at each end of next row, dec 1 [1, 1, 1, 1, 2] sts at each end of next row, dec 0 [0, 0, 1, 1,1] st at each end of next row, dec 0 [1, 1, 1, 1, 1] st at each end of next row. (24 [26, 28, 28, 30, 30] sts at end of last row)

Next rows: Continue working even in pattern until piece measures 6½ [7, 7, 7, 7½, 7½] inches from beg of Armhole Shaping.

FIRST SHOULDER

Last row: Work in established pattern across first 6 [6, 7, 6, 7, 7] sts, leaving rem sts unworked. Fasten off.

2ND SHOULDER

Last row: Sk next 12 [14, 14, 16, 16, 16] sts, join with sc in sp before next st, work in pattern across. Fasten off.

FIRST FRONT

Row 1: With size I hook, [ch 1, sc in back bar of ch] 15 [17, 19, 21, 23, 25] times, turn.

Row 2: Beg single love knot in first st, single love knot in each st across, turn.

Next rows: Rep row 2 until piece measures 12 [12, 12, 13, 13, 13] inches from beg.

ARMHOLE SHAPING

Next row: Mark beg of row for armhole edge, sl st across to sp before 3rd [3rd, 4th, 4th, 4th, 4th] sc, beg single love knot, single love knot across, leaving last 2 sts unworked, mark this end for neck edge, turn. (12 [14, 15, 17, 19, 21] sts)

Next rows: Continue in pattern and at same time using

beg single love knot dec and single love knot dec, dec 1 [1, 1, 1, 2, 2] sts at armhole edge of next row, dec 0 [0, 0, 1, 1, 2] sts at armhole edge and dec 1 st at neck edge of next row, dec 1 [1, 1, 1, 1, 2] sts at armhole edge on next row, dec 0 [0, 0, 1, 1, 1] st at armhole edge and dec 1 st at neck edge of next row, dec 0 [1, 1, 1, 1, 1] st at armhole edge on next row. *(8 [9, 10, 10, 11, 11] sts at end of last row)*

Next rows: Continue working in pattern at same time dec 1 st at neck edge on next row, then dec 1 st on neck edge every other row 1 [2, 2, 3, 3, 3] times. *(6 [6, 7, 6, 7, 7] sts at end of last row)*

Next rows: Continue working in established pattern until piece measures same as Back. At end of last row, fasten off.

2ND FRONT
Row 1: With size I hook, [ch 1, sc in back bar of ch] 15 [17, 19, 21, 23, 25] times, turn.

Row 2: Beg single love knot in first st, single love knot in each st across, turn.

Next rows: Rep row 2 until piece measures 12 [12, 12, 13, 13, 13] inches from beg.

ARMHOLE SHAPING
Next row: Mark beg of row for neck edge, beg single love knot dec, single love knot across, leaving

last 2 [2, 3, 3, 3, 3] sts unworked, mark this end for armhole edge, turn. *(12 [14, 15, 17, 19, 21] sts)*

Next rows: Work same as First Front.

SLEEVE
Make 2.
Row 1: With size I hook, [ch 1, sc in back bar of ch] 22 [24, 27, 29, 32, 34] times, turn.

Rows 2–4: Beg single love knot in first st, single love knot in each st across, turn.

CAP SHAPING
Next row: Sl st across to sp before 3rd [3rd, 4th, 4th, 4th, 4th] sc, beg single love knot, single love knot across, leaving last 3 [3, 3, 3, 3, 3] sts unworked, turn. *(18 [20, 21, 23, 26, 28] sts)*

Next rows: Continue working in established pattern and at same time using beg single love knot dec and single love knot dec, dec 1 st at each end of next 2 [2, 2, 2, 2, 3] rows, work 4 [4, 4, 3, 2, 1] rows even, dec 1 st at each end of next 4 [4, 4, 5, 6, 6] rows. At end of last row, fasten off. *(6 [8, 9, 9, 10, 10] sts at end of last row)*

FINISHING
Sew shoulder seams.

Fold 1 Sleeve in half lengthwise, place fold at Sleeve seam, sew in place.

Rep with rem Sleeve.

Sew side and Sleeve seams.

EDGING
Rnd 1: With size H hook, join with sc at seam, evenly sp sc around, join with sl st in beg sc.

Rnd 2: Working from left to right, **reverse sc** *(see Fig. 3)* in each st around, join with sl st in beg reverse sc. Fasten off.

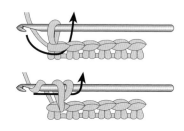

**Reverse Single Crochet
Fig. 3**

Work Edging around outer edge of Cover Up.

Work Edging around each Sleeve.

BUTTON LOOP
With size I hook, join with sl st to right Front at beg of neck edge, [ch 1, sc in back bar of ch] 4 times. Leaving long end for sewing, fasten off.

Sew end to same st as joining.

Sew button to left Front opposite Button Loop. ●

TOLL-FREE ORDER LINE or to request a free catalog (800) LV-ANNIE (800) 582-6643
Customer Service (800) AT-ANNIE (800) 282-6643, **Fax** (800) 882-6643
Visit AnniesAttic.com

We have made every effort to ensure the accuracy and completeness of these instructions.
We cannot, however, be responsible for human error, typographical mistakes or variations in individual work.

ISBN: 978-1-59635-182-0

Printed in USA

1 2 3 4 5 6 7 8 9

STITCH GUIDE

For more complete information, visit **AnniesAttic.com**

Abbreviations

beg	begin/beginning
bpdc	back post double crochet
bpsc	back post single crochet
bptr	back post treble crochet
CC	contrasting color
ch	chain stitch
ch-	refers to chain or space previously made (i.e., ch-1 space)
ch sp	chain space
cl	cluster
cm	centimeter(s)
dc	double crochet
dec	decrease/decreases/decreasing
dtr	double treble crochet
fpdc	front post double crochet
fpsc	front post single crochet
fptr	front post treble crochet
g	gram(s)
hdc	half double crochet
inc	increase/increases/increasing
lp(s)	loop(s)
MC	main color
mm	millimeter(s)
oz	ounce(s)
pc	popcorn
rem	remain/remaining
rep	repeat(s)
rnd(s)	round(s)
RS	right side
sc	single crochet
sk	skip(ped)
sl st	slip stitch
sp(s)	space(s)
st(s)	stitch(es)
tog	together
tr	treble crochet
trtr	triple treble crochet
WS	wrong side
yd(s)	yard(s)
yo	yarn over

Chain—ch: Yo, pull through lp on hook.

Slip stitch—sl st: Insert hook in st, pull through both lps on hook.

Single crochet—sc: Insert hook in st, yo, pull through st, yo, pull through both lps on hook.

Front post stitch—fp: Back post stitch—bp: When working post st, insert hook from right to left around post st on previous row.

Back   Front

Front loop—front lp Back loop— back lp

Front Loop   Back Loop

Half double crochet—hdc: Yo, insert hook in st, yo, pull through st, yo, pull through all 3 lps on hook.

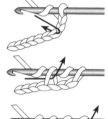

Double crochet—dc: Yo, insert hook in st, yo, pull through st, [yo, pull through 2 lps] twice.

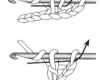

Change colors: Drop first color; with 2nd color, pull through last 2 lps of st.

Treble crochet—tr: Yo twice, insert hook in st, yo, pull through st, [yo, pull through 2 lps] 3 times.

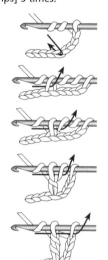

Double treble crochet—dtr: Yo 3 times, insert hook in st, yo, pull through st, [yo, pull through 2 lps], 4 times.

Single crochet decrease (sc dec): (Insert hook, yo, draw lp through) in each of the sts indicated, yo, draw through all lps on hook.

Half double crochet decrease (hdc dec): (Yo, insert hook, yo, draw lp through) in each of the sts indicated, yo, draw through all lps on hook.

Double crochet decrease (dc dec): (Yo, insert hook, yo, draw loop through, draw through 2 lps on hook) in each of the sts indicated, yo, draw through all lps on hook.

Treble crochet decrease (tr dec): Holding back last lp of each st, tr in each of the sts indicated, yo, pull through all lps on hook.

US		UK
sl st (slip stitch)	=	sc (single crochet)
sc (single crochet)	=	dc (double crochet)
hdc (half double crochet)	=	htr (half treble crochet)
dc (double crochet)	=	tr (treble crochet)
tr (treble crochet)	=	dtr (double treble crochet)
dtr (double treble crochet)	=	ttr (triple treble crochet)
skip	=	miss